Walton, Roger

686.224
D631
2

D0602228

Do-it-Yourself
Graphic Design

CONSULTANT EDITOR: JOHN LAING

Facts On File Publications
460 Park Avenue South
New York, N.Y. 10016

ART CENTER COLLEGE OF DESIGN

3 3220 00011 3865

CONTENTS

Do-it-Yourself Graphic Design

Copyright © 1984 by Swallow Publishing Limited

All rights reserved. No part of this book may be reproduced or utilized in any form or by any means, electronic or mechanical, including photocopying, recording or by any information storage and retrieval systems, without permission in writing from the Publisher.

Conceived and produced by
Swallow Publishing Limited
32 Hermes Street, London N1

Editor: Sarah Snape
Copy Editor: Mary Trewby
Designer: Caroline Courtenay
Illustrators: Steve Braund
           Neil MacCallum
Picture researcher: Liz Eddison
Colour photography: John Ridley

Published in the United States of America by Facts On File, Inc.
460 Park Avenue South, New York, N.Y. 10016

Published in Great Britain by Ebury Press

Library of Congress Cataloging in Publication Data
Main entry under title:

Do-it-yourself graphic design

Includes index
1. Printing, Practical – Amateur's manuals
2. Graphic arts – Amateur's manuals. I. Facts on File, Inc.
Z244.3. D6   1983   686.2'24   83-1526

ISBN 0-87196-474-0

Printed and bound in Spain

10 9 8 7 6 5 4 3 2 1

Here are just some examples of the wide range and application of graphic design. All of them are well within the range of the competent amateur; their professional appearance is a result of no more than simple hard work, a certain amount of trial and error, and of course a degree of skill – which can easily be yours.

Numerous aspects of design are displayed here: handwriting, dry transfer lettering, typesetting; drawings, photographs and illustrations; screen printing, lino-cuts and offset lithography. Note how the designs complement their subject, and how inappropriate some would look if changed around – the handwritten cover of the directory of local poetry groups, for example, with the savings brochure below it.

All of these effects can be achieved by anyone with a little patience, practical aptitude and imagination – and, of course, the skills and knowledge that this book can bring you.

INTRODUCTION

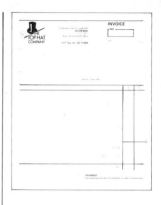

To most people, the word 'design' conjures up images of creative young men and women working through the night to produce glamorous, full-colour advertisements. But advertisements are only a tiny proportion of the items produced by graphic designers: most are not working on expensive campaigns for multinational companies, but doing careful, meticulous work in cramped studios, producing such everyday items as tax forms and telephone bills, books and wall charts, newspapers and stamps, airline tickets and bank notes, greeting cards and letterheads – anything, in fact, that is printed. The work of the graphic designer is, simply, to ensure that a given piece of information is communicated as clearly and as effectively as possible.

In the past, design was only one aspect of a craftsman's work; the object had to be executed, and then sold as well. But as printing became more mechanized and demands for printed material grew, a division of skills developed between the printer and the designer. Graphic communication developed into an independent and essential discipline.

In the past thirty years, dramatic technical advances have been made in design equipment, and in reproduction and printing techniques. The tools and materials now available in art shops and good stationers enable anyone with just a little practical aptitude to produce professional-looking material quickly, simply and cheaply. Perfect circles, curves and straight lines are drawn easily with stencils, flexicurves and French curves; colour is applied evenly with felt-tip pens and markers, or self-adhesive coloured film; stencils or dry-transfer lettering produce calligraphic and other decorative letterforms in seconds; and, instead of ruining a piece of work, a slip of the pen can be instantly eradicated with a bleach pen or correction fluid. Modern type-writers can print type that almost passes for

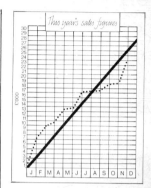

typesetting, and the development of the polaroid camera has even given us a source of instant pictures. Exciting and colourful binding materials are also cheaply available, making it easy to present information in a modern and professional way.

But even more important are the huge leaps that have been made in the fields of reproduction and printing, notably the development of phototypesetting, small offset litho machines and sophisticated photocopiers Thanks to the boom in instant print shops, these machines are now accessible to all of us, making it easier than ever before to get cheap, good quality printed material.

As soon as you realise that design is not just the domain of the trained and talented, endless possibilities open up. With a few tools and materials – pens, cardboard and paper, a typewriter, stencils or dry transfer lettering, some tracing paper, and inks or coloured papers – you can produce your own letterhead, Christmas cards or For Sale notice. If you are a teacher, you can make exciting and stimulating material for the classroom – friezes, wall charts, pictures and diagrams. Or you could produce banners, leaflets, magazines and posters for a community or political group you are involved with. The owners of small businesses can create their own 'image' cheaply with impressive stationery and packaging, while teenagers will enjoy printing T-shirts and invitations, or publicity material.

The secret of graphic design is not to be afraid of cheating. Trace off designs you like in books and use them to draw illustrations. Cut pictures out of magazines and paste them down on your cards. Copy or adapt ideas wherever you see them (you will soon start developing your own). And, above all, use all the tricks and devices we describe in this book – they are the 'trade secrets' of every professional designer.

GLOSSARY

Align To arrange letters on a vertical or horizontal line.

Baseline The horizontal line the type sits on.

Bold Type which has a heavy black appearance.

Cast off To calculate how much space a particular amount of copy will take in a given type size and measure.

Centred type Type which is positioned in the centre of the image area or type measure.

Character A single letter, punctuation mark or space cast in type.

Character count The number of characters in a given amount of copy.

Colour of type The appearance of type on the page, dependent on the line spacing. The more space, the paler the type will look.

Colour separation The process by which an image is separated into two or more plates for printing – one for each colour.

Condensed face A typeface which has a narrow squashed-up appearance.

Continuous tone Unscreened photograph or illustration containing tone gradations from black through to white.

Dry transfer lettering A form of letter generation in which letters are transferred by burnishing from a sheet to artwork.

Duotone A process in which one image is printed from two negatives, one concentrating on the darker shades with greater detail, the other on the lighter flat tint.

Em A unit of measurement used in printing, equal to the square of the point size of the type being used.

En A unit, half the width of an em, used in printing.

Expanded type A typeface which has a flattened, wide appearance.

Family The term used to describe the different weights of a typeface, e.g. Bembo bold, Bembo medium, Bembo italic.

Filmsetting The process of using photographic methods for composition.

Font A collective term for all the available characters in one member of a family of type eg. Univers *bold*.

Grid A guide used by designers to organise the elements on a page in a consistent manner. It shows column widths, picture areas etc.

GSM (grams per square metre) A unit of measurement for paper (weights).

Halftone A process by which continuous tone is simulated by reducing the image to be printed into a series of dots of varying sizes.

Hatching A series of lines in an illustration which gives the illusion of tones.

Hot metal A general term for type cast from molten metal.

Image The type or illustration to be reproduced by printing.

Imposition The arrangement of pages of artwork so that when printed and folded the text will be in the correct order.

Impression All the copies of a book printed during the same print run.

Justification Spacing of words so that lines in a column are of equal length.

Layout A rough sketch which indicates how text and illustration will relate to each other on the printed page.

Leaded type Type which has been set with lead (or space) between the lines.

Letterpress A printing process in which the image on the printing plate is raised and inked to produce an impression.

Line up To align two pieces of type or illustration vertically or horizontally.

Lithography A printing process based on the principle of the mutual repulsion of water and oil. The printing plate is dampened and greasy ink is used.

Lower case The small letters (non-capitals) in a font of type.

Mark-up To instruct the typesetter or printer what to do with the copy or illustrations supplied.

Measure The maximum width of a line of type.

Medium A weight of typeface between bold and light; often referred to as Roman.

Offset lithography A printing method in which the image is 'offset' on to a rubber-covered cylinder or plate and then printed.

Overlay A covering for artwork on which instructions are written. Also a transparent sheet used in the preparation of multi-coloured artwork.

Page proofs Proofs of type which has been set in blocks as it will appear on the printed page.

Photo-lithography A printing method in which the image is transferred to the plate photographically, and then 'offset'.

Pica The unit of measurement used in typesetting. One pica equals 12 points.

Point The standard unit for measuring type size, equal to approximately 0.3 mm (1/72 inch).

Proof A trial impression of copy or an illustration obtained before printing in order to check accuracy.

Register The alignment of two or more plates used to print one page or image.

Reproduction proofs (repro) High-quality proofs which can be used as artwork.

Roman Ordinary, vertical type; often referred to as medium.

Screen A screen of dots on a halftone; the higher the number, the finer the reproduction will be.

Serif The small decorative stroke at the ends of the main body of a character. This book is set in a serif typeface. A typeface which has no serifs is called sans serif.

Set solid Typesetting with no line leading.

Signature The individual sections of pages which make up a book. They are always divisible by 4; usually a signature is of 16 pages.

Upper case The capital letters in a font of type.

Weight The different styles within one typeface, eg. light, medium, italic, bold and extra bold.

x height The height of the letter x in any typeface, used as a reference from which other measurements of a particular typeface can be taken.

1. A SHORT HISTORY OF GRAPHIC DESIGN

Graphic design is the translation of ideas and concepts into some sort of structural order and visual form. It is the art of books and magazines, advertising, packaging and propaganda.

The term 'graphic designer', coined by the American book designer William Addison Dwiggins, was not used until 1922. But examples of graphic art can be traced as far back as the Phoenicians, who invented a graphic representation of language in their alphabetical script during the second millenium BC. As the use of the written word became more widespread, the need for effective organisation of material created in turn a need for design. Early systems of writing, either in columns or across the page, demonstrate the use of a grid, however basic, to

The illustration above is taken from a graphic arts manual published in 1568. It shows a designer drawing an image in preparation for a woodcut or a copper engraving. His tools include callipers, a rule and engraving knives.

Until the fifteenth century all books were laboriously handwritten by scribes (left). Printing was first developed as a means of graphic reproduction by the German metalsmith Johann Gutenberg in the 1440s. Gutenberg introduced movable type, using the square compact Gothic lettering style common in Germany at the time as his style of lettering. He is depicted here in a Victorian print.

systematically divide up the page and facilitate communication.

The development of mechanical printing methods in the fifteenth century was a significant turning point. Only 30 years before Gutenberg first used movable type, Oxford University had just 121 manuscripts in its library: a book then was as valuable as an acre of land. But the

The English artist William Morris revived quality book production in the 1890s, using medieval and botanical forms as inspiration.

NOTE BY WILLIAM MORRIS ON HIS AIMS IN FOUNDING THE KELMSCOTT PRESS.

I BEGAN printing books with the hope of producing some which would have a definite claim to beauty, while at the same time they should be easy to read and should not dazzle the eye, or trouble the intellect of the reader by eccentricity of form in the letters. I have always been a great admirer of the calligraphy of the Middle Ages, & of the earlier printing which took its place. As to the fifteenth-century books, I had noticed that they were always beautiful by force of the mere typography, even without the added ornament, with which many of them are so lavishly supplied. And it was the essence of my undertaking to produce books which it would be a pleasure to look upon as pieces of printing and arrangement of type. Looking at my adventure from this point of view then, I found I had to consider chiefly the following things: the paper, the form of the type, the relative spacing of the letters, the words, and the

development of mechanical printing meant that soon great quantities of books and pamphlets became widely available.

The nineteenth century was a great watershed for design in Britain. The Industrial Revolution, together with the development of the lithographic printing process, had led to an immense increase in the amount of printed material, and to a corresponding decrease in the standard of book design and production. In 1890, as a reaction against the poor quality of mass-produced products of the time, the socialist artist and writer William Morris set up the Kelmscott Press to print beautiful handcrafted volumes. Morris's main inspirations were medieval and botanical forms, his designs naturalistic with formal borders. He designed three highly decorative typefaces – Golden, Troy and Chaucer – which, although still available today, are no longer widely used. A contemporary of his, Aubrey Beardsley, developed the design ideas of the Kelmscott Press further by synthesizing them – much to Morris's fury – with the style of Japanese wood-block prints, working in black and white to further stress the contrast between the natural and the geometric. Beardsley's work was enthusiastically received and he became the art editor for *The Yellow Book,* an avant-garde London arts magazine.

Another important designer of the time was Charles Ricketts, who criticised Beardsley's work on the grounds that it was confined to illustrations which were slotted into manuscript. Ricketts believed that a book should be designed as a total entity, aiming for a harmony between all its elements inside and out. Ricketts set up the Vale Press, and produced a number of beautifully designed volumes.

Beardsley and Ricketts were both part of the Art Nouveau movement, which originated in France at the end of the nineteenth century. Art Nouveau was a synthesis of European art and the Japanese print, which had first become known in

One of the foremost artists of the late nineteenth century Art Nouveau movement was Henri Toulouse-Lautrec. Although primarily a painter, he is best remembered for his posters which depict Parisian nightlife during la belle epoque. The posters were a milestone in graphic design, creating dynamic shapes and patterns by the use of blocks of colour, flat silhouettes and stylized drawing techniques.

Until his death at the age of twenty-six, Aubrey Beardsley was regarded as the enfant terrible of the English Art Nouveau movement. He created his striking images by synthesizing the style of Japanese wood-block prints with the design ideas of William Morris's Kelmscott Press, using black and white to contrast the geometric and the natural.

the West in the mid-nineteenth century. One of the foremost French practitioners of this movement was Henri Toulouse-Lautrec, who became famous for his posters depicting night-life in Paris. His posters used dynamic pattern and shape for their effect, adopting the same flat silhouettes, blocks of colour and stylized drawing techniques as the Japanese print. However, it was Alphonse Mucha, a Czech artist who came to study in Paris in 1887, who finally perfected the

Alphonse Mucha incorporated Art Nouveau motifs into his highly decorative and stylized posters (left).

The Bauhaus artist Joost Schmidt used abstract shapes and geometric grid systems in his posters (below).

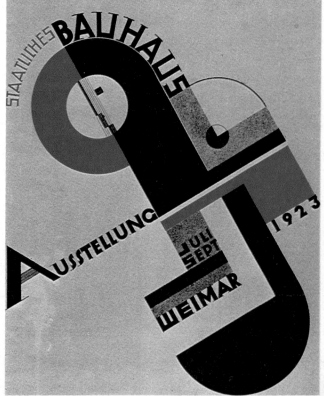

abcdefghijklmnopq rstuvwxyz .,;:?!-'&£ ABCDEFGHIJKLMN

The Futura typeface above was designed in Germany in the 1920s by Paul Renner. In all, 15 alphabets were designed in this new geometrical, sans-serif face.

A. M. Cassandre was the pseudonym used by Adolphe Mouron, the brilliant Russian immigrant of the 1920s, whose bold designs revitalized French posters.

Art Nouveau poster with his posters for Sarah Bernhardt's appearance in Gismonden and his advertisement for Job cigarette papers. His work had such an impact on the art world that the phrase 'le style Mucha' was sometimes interchanged with 'l'Art Nouveau'.

The distinctive flowing organic forms and swirling patterns used by these artists were rejected by the major art movements of the early twentieth century. Influenced by the intense violence and turbulence in Europe in the first two decades of the century, Cubism, Futurism, Dada and Surrealism, and Russian Constructivism all had profound effects on the language of graphic design.

Closely associated with these painting styles was the Bauhaus school, which opened in Weimar in 1919. Its principal was the revolutionary architect Walter Gropius. In common with Futurism and Constructivism, and in contrast to William Morris, the Bauhaus attempted to bring industry and art together. They believed that industrialization presented an important opportunity to the artist, but that only the most brilliant ideas justified mass production. The Bauhaus introduced a large number of innovative ideas in graphic design as well as other areas, and the school's influence can be traced in many of the typographic practices still current today; for example, material organized in progression from the most important information down to subsidiary details, in type size and weight; and the widespread use of sans-serif typefaces.

An important figure of the 1930s was the German typographer Jan Tschichold, who embraced the ideas of the Bauhaus but produced his own, more refined style, incorporating photographs into designs where previously only illustrations had been used. He rejected decoration, concentrating instead on purely functional design. However, by the 1940s, Tschichold had revived a more humanist approach, using traditional typefaces; it was, he commented, 'genuine torture' to read pages of sans-serif type.

In the 1950s a design style called the International Typographical Style was developed by Swiss designers. They took Tschichold's methods of the 1930s a step further with their clean academic approach, and one of today's most popular typefaces – Univers – can be ascribed to their movement. Legibility and order were the ideal, and to achieve this sans-serif typefaces, mathematically drawn grids and factual copy and photographs were used. A particularly influential innovation was the asymmetrical alignment of copy on one side of a column, known as unjustified, or ragged, type (see page 42).

In the meantime, the art centre of the world had shifted from Europe to New York, where the Americans were developing their own original graphic design styles. American designers displayed a more intuitive, pragmatic approach than their formal European counterparts. Emphasis was placed on originality and novelty. Designers sought to present information in an open, direct way, yet simultaneously, to express their own personal ideas. Collage and montage, handwriting and symbols were among the elements combined by the followers of what has been called the American School of Graphic Expressionism.

At the same time, the work of Pop artists reflected an upsurge in social awareness and the search for alternative lifestyles. Rock groups, psychedelic drugs and anti-establishment slogans became the themes of Pop art posters, which also protested against the war, repression, anti-feminism and other social injustices. By 1960 there was a greater stress on the symbolic elements in design and a more widespread design consciousness.

The Swiss-based Post Modernist movement flourished in the 1970s. The clinical look of the International Typographical Style was

FRANK SINATRA · ELEANOR PARKER · KIM NOVAK

THE MAN WITH THE GOLDEN ARM

A FILM BY OTTO PREMINGER

rethought, and some of the spontaneity of American design with its rich visual effects was employed. Paragraphs were no longer indented, type weights were changed in mid-word, wide letterspacing was used and new typography was designed in response to new technology.

Since the Second World War, the boundaries of graphic design have broadened to include, as well as the traditional individual designer, large industrial corporations and flourishing advertising agencies. Advertising and corporate images now play an important role in graphic art, and today, in the electronic age, computer graphics, system design and media graphics constitute an exciting new language, the full potential of which is still not fully understood. The task of the graphic designer will continue to be as challenging in the future as it has been in the past.

The poster's stark abstract design (opposite) reflects the film's theme of drug addiction. It was produced by Saul Bass, a leading artist in the 1950s New York School.

This Bob Dylan poster (left) perfectly expresses the anti-establishment and psychedelic themes of much of the rock culture in the late 1960s.

An example of the newest medium for the graphic designer: high resolution computer graphics, using type and illustration combined.

2. GRAPHIC DESIGN – HOW IT WORKS

This century, the number and availability of consumer goods and services has increased to such an extent that all the products have to compete fiercely with each other for a share of the market. This competition has encouraged the growth of advertising and the proliferation of images and words exhorting us to notice 'this' as opposed to 'that'.

In the course of a day, or even a few hours, the number of words we see is colossal. But, despite this profusion, we usually know how to extract or impose sense upon what we see. And yet it appears in an unordered way, in a sequence over which we have no control. So how does it communicate?

On a short walk through a neighbourhood street in any large city the 'word world' reveals itself in all its chaos – and its order. You would probably notice significantly less than 1 per cent of the words you passed, so even without realizing it, you have already exercised a large degree of selection and simplification. The sample given below is presented in the order in which the words turned up: there is no arranged relationship between them. In fact, they read like nonsense:

Beware of the dog. Volkswagen. No parking in front of this garage, please. Passengers must not cross the line. The taste that was born in a can won't die in the fridge. Black together. The Half Moon. Luncheons. Save without struggle. Shell. The Crusty Cob. McDonalds. Grand Wrestling Spectacular. 'Cyanide' Sid Johnson v. Winston 'The Bear' Nelson. In our business the customer is king. Person required 5 mornings a week to help with food. Amoco. He that buys eggs buys many shells. The ultimate elegance in mohair and wool. Palmist: Love, Career, Illness. All aspects of your life covered and guidance given. Prudential Insurance. Californian nuts. The Love of God be with you. Bowie!

How do we cope with this extraordinary onslaught? Apart from one or two familiar phrases, the words are not very informative.

Visual meaning and association

As a result of this confusion it is tempting to say that in these kinds of circumstances we 'see' the words but don't 'read' them. But if the rate of bombardment is intense enough then, even if we are not very aware of what we are seeing, the message ultimately strikes home. That is why the degree of familiarity with slogans and trade symbols is so high. And the visual identity of certain names and products is particularly strong; so much so that even given only a small part of the 'image' it can be quite easy to accurately identify the source. Someone seeing a portion of a sign, the letters 'Co' in white on red, for example, will recognize them as belonging to a Coca Cola advertisement.

This progression is possible simply because we have become used to associating a certain style of lettering with Coca Cola. Even a partial glimpse of the image is enough to arouse a memory of the company that uses the image.

Many factors act as triggers for meaning and association. It isn't just what the words say, or what the name is, that counts. It is the whole environment that builds up into providing clues to identify a product or manufacturer.

There is far more to a trade name than just the name itself. In the random selection of words seen on the walk, there were two names associated with oil companies, Shell and Amoco. If asked to associate each of these with one of the two shapes and colours given here, most people would make the correct association.

Despite having very little to go on, you have seen these signs so often that you are able to associate the name with the image.

The way in which information is presented, and the circumstances in which it is presented, are extremely important. If the context or the surroundings are unfamiliar, the results can be obscure, misleading or comical. Look, for example, at the familiar name presented in an unfamiliar context bottom right of this page.

Symbols alone (right) are recognizable. Something is obviously wrong (far right) when Volkswagen and Rolls-Royce symbols are mixed.

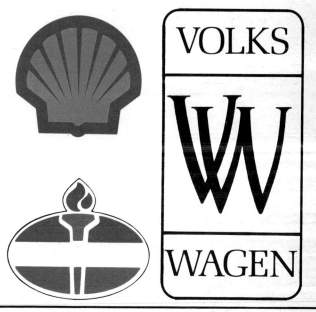

We readily associate a product's name and graphic image with each other (above and right). Even a portion of a brand name immediately suggests the product.

Choosing the design to suit the message

But it is not only certain names or companies that have acquired specific visual identities. Whole *areas* of working and social life have visual associations, styles and identities. The sober respectability of a lawyer is in contrast with the up-market image of a rock music promoter or the direct, no-nonsense approach of a transport operator. This difference is reflected in any graphic material they may use in their working lives (see chapter 5). If unexpected forms of presentation are used, the results are immediately seen to be incongruous.

In order to convey information successfully it is essential that the most appropriate style is chosen for the subject. In these examples the desired effect is lost because the style used creates the wrong impression about the subject. The image of sober respectability normally associated with doctors is entirely lost in the brazen and loud sign used here, while the solicitor's sign is far too flippant and off-hand. Similarly the computer sign is too flowery – a more clinical and straightforward style would be more appropriate.

Arranging the design elements

We all know how language is organized: words form sentences, which follow certain rules of grammar. Sentences knit together to become paragraphs, and so on. But what are the principles of visual organization?

Graphic design is, essentially, a two-dimensional activity involving the arrangement of shapes on a surface, usually flat, which has boundaries on the left and right, and on the top and bottom.

The events that occur on this surface fall into two categories: words and pictures. 'Words' means, possibly, only one word, or a headline of several words, or a longer piece of text. 'Pictures' includes photographs, drawings, illustrations, or just simple abstract shapes that may have little or no meaning outside the context of the particular surface.

Designing with style

Imagine you have to design a poster for a wrestling match. The words (or *copy*) to go on this poster are: Wrestling Spectacular. 'Cyanide' Sid Johnson v. Winston 'The Bear' Nelson. The Municipal Hall. 8 June.

Even using only the simplest printing methods, this copy can be presented in a range of ways which give visual expression to the activity being publicized, as well as informing the public, by using the words in the normal way.

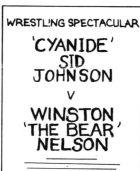

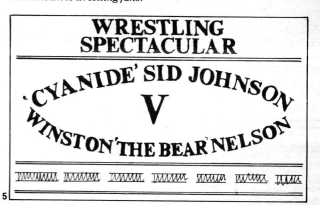

There are so many ways of choosing and arranging the different elements of a message. Sketch out ideas until you find the most effective solution.

1. It conveys some information, but not enough to interest a casual observer.

2. This makes some feature of the names of the contenders which, by their highly colourful nature, suggests that they are well known to wrestling fans.

3. This makes more of these names, but it isn't clear what kind of event is taking place.

4. This brings out the wrestling aspect, but the personalities have got lost.

5. This begins to combine the sense of the activity and the identity of the combatants, using only common letterforms.

Solving a design problem

Two important design factors are scale and colour – these are applied when designing a road sign, which must be clear and unequivocable.

The elements involved in the message are, simply:
1. A surface.
2. The information on the surface.
3. The scale of this information.
4. The colour of this information.

1. The surface:

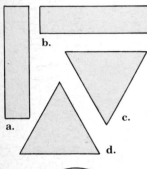

2. The information on the surface: *'STOP'*.

3. The scale of this information:

The letters are too small. No matter what size, the sign would not have sufficient impact.

Small (lower case) letters with a capital are easier to read. But lower case letters are not 'urgent' enough.

The letters are now too large for the surface. They crowd the shape and are difficult to read.

The size of the letters is good. The message can be easily read by drivers of vehicles that may be moving at high speed.

This is more eye-catching, but, although the lettering would be readable at night, the sign itself would not be seen.

4. The colour of this information:

An obvious mistake; the sign is not noticeable and its message is not readable.

Certainly eye-catching and can be easily seen day and night, but it is difficult to read and does not convey a sense of danger.

It is readable but is not eye-catching.

It is eye-catching and readable in day and night conditions. Because it uses red, there is the association with danger.

a. *Impractical: the shape is too slender to catch the eye.*

b. *Even more difficult than the first example.*

c. *Possible, but the triangular shape makes the placing of the letters difficult.*

d. *Another possibility, but, again, the placing of the letters is difficult unless the sign is very large, in which case they will begin to get lost within the surface.*

e. *Better. The letters can be contained and it is well proportioned for use at the roadside.*

Adding pictures

The example opposite uses only one word and a few simple layout and colour variations. With pictures, the range of opportunities open to the designer becomes much wider and even more subtle. A fantastic spectrum of reactions and recognitions can be invoked by persuasive visual statements (sometimes called visual rhetoric).

For example, cars are advertised photographically in two basic ways. The first suggests a flawless machine incorporating the most up-to-date technology. It is presented in a rather detached scientific manner. Possession of this remote and mysterious machine, which has qualities some of us aspire to, it is suggested, would make us envied and, somehow, impregnable to any criticism or attack.

The other approach underlines the rôle of the car in a stable and satisfactory family: life could not be other than a self-fulfilled dream if we possess this car. The photographs show relaxed husbands/fathers, satisfied and content wives/mothers and healthy, vibrant children whose journey through life is going to be immeasurably aided by the reassuring driveability and safety of the car.

Without the photographs, it all sounds a little ridiculous, even far-fetched. But look at the photographs: they underwrite the values and feelings just considered very skilfully.

With thoughtful manipulation, you can get an image to do far more than simply illustrate an outward form. That is fairly obvious if applied to photographs and illustrations. But the same effect can be obtained purely with lettering.

Who can do without the luxury car (above)? Especially when it is the most up-to-date technical dream car ever, with its sleekness and speed. Note how the photograph emphasizes the machine's superiority to any other, underlining the qualities a potential owner will automatically possess – power, money, exquisite taste. In the second example (right), the carefully contrived scene is intended to suggest that this car is somehow integral to the family and is absolutely essential for its happy and contented future.

3.WHERE DO YOU START?

Before you tackle your first design project, it is important to define exactly what the purpose of your task is. The most obvious way of dealing with it is not necessarily the best. It may, in fact, be quite wrong because you have failed to take into account *all* the aspects of the situation.

No matter how simple a problem appears to be, it is advisable to define it carefully, using a simple check-list:

1. *What* do you want to achieve; what is your objective?
2. *Who* is the message aimed at?
3. *What* needs to be said?
4. *How* are you going to convey the message?

Notice that the question of 'how?' is *last* on this list.

1. *What do you want to achieve?*

Is any graphic object required at all? It may be that a few well-placed telephone calls will achieve your objective. Do you wish to inform people of some event, explain a complicated theory or idea, promote some political, social or religious point of view; or do you wish, simply, to entertain?

2. *Who is the message aimed at?*

Presumably you have a particular audience in mind. How large is this audience? What age group? Both sexes, or only one? Where is this audience: local; country-wide; international? Do they have anything in common – children at the same school; smoke cigarettes; own their own homes?

3. *What needs to be said?*

Defining the nature and size of the audience helps to decide what needs to be said. For example, the instruction sheet in a public telephone box does not need to describe and explain the workings inside the instrument. It simply needs to tell how, when and where to put in your money and how and when you should dial a number. Conversely, the manual required by the telephone company's maintenance engineer does not need to explain how to use the telephone but it must describe all the working parts inside, how they relate to each other, and how to establish that they are in effective working order.

4. *How are you going to convey the message?*

By now one particular kind of print should begin to suggest itself as the best and most logical way of answering your needs. If you decide to produce a poster, you do so not because you happen to like posters but because a poster is going to meet your need more effectively than anything else.

Case history 1: Directing different groups to a conference and exhibition centre

1. What do you want to achieve?
The object is to explain to various groups of people in different parts of the world how to get to a conference and exhibition centre in New York.

2. Who is the message aimed at?
Possible audiences might be:
a. A delivery man who lives within 3 km (1¾ miles) of the conference centre.
b. A specialist crew of 12 who will mount an exhibition associated with a conference. Each member will travel individually from New Jersey.
c. 500 delegates coming to the conference from all over the world.
d. The 20,000 members of the public from America, Canada and Europe who will visit the exhibition.

3. What needs to be said?
a. How to travel by road from the depot to the conference centre.

b. How to get to New York by road and rail, and how to find the centre once in New York.
c. Air travel details from major international airports, plus local directions from the two airports in New York to the conference centre.
d. All of the above.

4. How are you going to convey the message?
a. There is only one person to deal with: no printed material need be produced. A rough sketch is all that is necessary.
b. A collective briefing with maps and directions to be supplemented with supporting material for each individual, such as a handwritten or typewritten sheet of basic instructions (with or without a map), which has been photocopied or duplicated.
c. For the first time in this analysis, the number of people being instructed warrants the use of printed material. Since it will have to be printed, it might

be economical to combine travel details with details of the conference itself: a timetable, a list of speakers, arrangements for accommodation etc. All this could be attractively displayed in a leaflet or booklet.

d. A leaflet or a section in a trade journal or other relevant publication would be the best solution.

Costing

Instruction sheets: If 250 or fewer copies are required then duplicating or photocopying is cheaper than printing. Duplicating is very cheap but the technique has been largely superseded by photocopying,

When preparing material think of the whole range that will be needed. In this example, a local delivery man will need fewer and simpler instructions than an executive coming to the conference from Europe.

which is also cheap. As with all printing methods, the greater the number of copies the cheaper the unit cost becomes.

Leaflets: If more than 250 copies are needed then look carefully at the comparative costs of photocopying and

printing. At about this number printing begins to become cheaper. There are inexpensive print centres, similar to photocopying shops, in most large towns. Larger professional printers will also handle this kind of work, but they are likely to be more expensive because their overheads tend to be higher.

Booklets: The printing and distribution of booklets is a complex and expensive undertaking. It is vital to ask at least three printers to give you a quotation, with a detailed breakdown of how much they would charge for

each part of the printing process (paper, printing, binding, etc.). For various reasons there can be quite a difference between the prices printers charge for doing the same job. In this case, distribution would be relatively simple: either by hand, or by post (for which you must allow the cost of stamps and envelopes).

This case history has offered several fairly clear cut circumstances. Frequently it is not so simple and there are several alternatives, all of which seem equally practical.

Case history 2: Publicizing an independent theatre

1. What do you want to achieve?
In order to stay in business you must make a profit. To do this, you must fill your theatre – so that is the objective.

2. Who is the message aimed at?
As many of the potential audience as possible. Not everyone can or wants to go to the theatre. Or they may be interested only in some of the plays being shown. So the potential audience must be identified. It will depend on the type of play you are showing. For example, possible audiences might be:
a. People interested in situation comedies and musical extravaganzas.
b. People who enjoy contemporary, political plays, or 'alternative' theatre.
c. People who want to see traditional theatre, such as Beckett or Shakespeare.

3. What needs to be said?
Which plays are on and when (and at what times); membership details (if necessary), and the prices of admission. In addition, you would need to give a brief description of the plays and who directed and acted in them.

4. How are you going to convey the message?
The local newspaper is the most obvious place to advertise. But if you advertise every day and/or if you use display advertisements it will be expensive.

The advantage of 'taking space' in a newspaper is that you are reaching a very wide potential audience. But is it the right audience? If you do use newspapers, use your judgement and be as selective as possible when deciding when or where to advertise.

Another way of reaching a general audience is to produce a poster. This need not be too expensive, and one poster could easily cover a week's showings and possibly a month's programmes.

The disadvantage of the poster is that it will reach a smaller audience than the newspaper. Will it reach as many people as you need? If you select the best sites – for instance, a display space adjacent to a theatre bookstore – posters can be an excellent and inexpensive method of advertising.

Another technique is a small leaflet produced in large numbers. Such a leaflet may use only an eighth of the paper you would need for a poster, so about 800 leaflets could be produced at a similar price as 100 posters. (For various technical reasons (see chapter 10), the number could be significantly over 1,000.)

Again, the best places to have these leaflets on offer must be carefully judged, and depend on the kind of plays you are showing: the theatre itself; libraries; colleges; certain bookstores and record stores, for example, might be the most suitable.

Of course, other non-visual techniques can be used: a telephone answering machine which repeats the salient information to any caller is

very efficient and reasonably priced. Or buy time on a local radio channel: a lot can be said in 10 seconds.

Costing

Advertising: Usually terms for advertising can be negotiated with newspapers and magazines. For example, if from time to time you take a small display space (one which is bigger than a mere listing in the entertainments column) they will often allow you the ordinary listing at a discount rate. The same applies to radio advertising.

Posters: If you only require up to 50 posters, then screen-printing (see chapter 10) is the best technique. If a larger number, then you should consider lithographic printing (chapter 10).

It is cheaper to print in one colour only. This colour need not be black – it is immaterial to a printer what colour ink is being used; what is important is how many times the article being printed must go through the press (it only prints one colour at a time). This is why printers refer to any print run as a *printing* and not as a colour.

If you do use an ink other than black, use a dark colour, otherwise the lettering and typesetting are difficult to read and any photographic reproductions tend to disappear altogether.

Leaflets: A local print shop will give you very favourable rates. Again, think only of printing in one colour.

Typesetting: There are various ways of reproducing your text (see chapters 4 and 8): you do not have to go to a large and prestigious, and therefore expensive, typesetting firm; there are smaller printers/ typesetters who will do your job more cheaply and as efficiently. One of the recent growth areas in letter generation has been

The illustration (opposite) was done in a popular, realistic technique, using a combination of inks and gouache. An ink base, put down with a large brush, provided a dark tone (varying in colour), then the illustration was worked up to its finished state.

the development of typewriter composition techniques. Some of these produce letter images that are virtually indistinguishable, except to the professional eye, from conventionally produced typesetting. Such techniques are much cheaper than conventional means. But any electric typewriter will produce perfectly acceptable 'typesetting' for your purposes. Whichever method you choose, you will have to assemble all the elements of your designs. The techniques required are explained in chapter 9.

4. GETTING DOWN TO DESIGN

VISUALIZING

Once you have decided upon the most appropriate medium for your message, you can get down to designing it. Making roughs – or visualizing – enables you to see what the design will look like before it is actually produced. Whatever the item may be, and regardless of whether it is photo-copied, printed or hand-made, initially it will need to be visualized. The process of producing roughs (sometimes called *scamps,* or *comps*) of a number of possible solutions and ideas helps make the necessary visual decisions.

POINTS TO REMEMBER

When visualizing, take the following factors into account:
1. The size, roughly, of the finished article (the final decision can be taken later).
2. The amount of copy (number of words) to be fitted into the space.
3. The number of pictures and diagrams to be used.
4. The appearance of the pictures and words.
5. Whether there is going to be colour. If so, how many colours?

Scaled-down roughs

If you are designing a small leaflet – say, using a sheet of either 210 x 297 mm, or 8½ x 11 inch paper folded in half – it is possible to plan rough ideas on a sheet of paper the same size. However, if you are working on a large size poster it would be quicker and cheaper to work out a rough on a smaller scale, but in proportion. When you work on a small scale it is not necessary to write out all the text and draw detailed illustrations. Full-size roughs can be done once you have more or less decided on what the final design will be.

Below are four scaled-down roughs (visuals)

A. Type is centred.

B. Type aligns on the left.

C. Type aligns on the right.

D. Tilted, left-aligned type.

for a flower show poster. Each rough contains the same components arranged in a different way and each word of type has been indicated by a pencil mark.

These roughs are a way of finding visual answers to the questions:
1. What is important in the message?
2. Where should the visual emphasis be?

The poster has no picture and is relying on type alone – which can be used in a number of different ways – to carry the information. The design decisions are to do with *weight* of type (that is, how big and dark it is) and where it is to be positioned.

Once you have decided which arrangement you like best, the visualizing can be taken a few stages further. Below are four roughs based on (A), although any of the others could be chosen. In the first one, the heading has been made larger and bolder. In the second example, the heading is larger but not bolder. The third one uses a handwritten heading, and the fourth takes the handwriting idea and combines it with the diagonal appearance of rough (D).

This process should be repeated, changing and moving the elements around until a satisfactory decision can be made.

The following alterations can be made to type:
1. The typeface (the shape of type).
2. The size of the type.
3. The spaces between the letters.
4. The spaces between the words.
5. The spaces between the lines.
6. The position and arrangement of the words and lines. That is, where the text falls on the page and whether it falls in lines of equal length (*justified*) or unequal length (*unjustified*).

There are obviously many ways to use type and the magnitude of possible solutions can make decisions hard to arrive at. Questions to ask about the final version of the flower show poster are:
1. Can it be seen from a distance? A poster needs larger type than a booklet, which in turn needs larger type than a letterhead.
2. Does the arrangement and style of the type reflect the nature of the message? A poster for a flower show should emphasize the natural, while one for a new technology exhibition, for example, should stress the mechanical.
3. Is it attractive to the audience it is aimed at (see chapter 3)?

1. Heading is larger.

2. Heading is larger, bolder.

3. 'Flowery' handwriting.

4. 'Flowery', tilted heading.

Full-size roughs

Having chosen the most successful rough, the next stage is to do a full-size version. This may suggest that further alterations to the design are necessary.

The flower show poster is an example of how just a few words and headings can be visualized; a programme of events for the flower show would involve many more. Even when visualizing, accuracy in representing how the words and pictures appear is important, and techniques for this are shown in chapter 8. Text can be represented on a rough by boxes and lines: it is not necessary to write everything out. A better impression of the general appearance of text and headings is given simply by different weights of line. Pictures are roughly represented with boxes.

SEVERAL WAYS TO REPRESENT TYPE

Instead of writing out the words when visualising, use different weights of pencil line to indicate the copy and give a general impression of how the text will appear.

The heading is written in full because of its size and because in this case the hand lettering is a special part of the whole design.

Pictures are indicated by boxes. You can draw a very rough sketch of the picture in the box or simply draw a diagonal cross.

Picture captions are usually typeset in smaller type than the text, so these are indicated by closer lines.

Subheadings are indicated by a heavy squiggle.

Text (or body type) is represented by constantly spaced lines.

A rough for the flower show programme using a combination of type and pictures, which have been arranged in three columns.

THE ELEMENTS OF DESIGN

The function of roughs is to show what the finished design will look like. But before making an accurate rough, you must know what production methods you will be using: on what type of paper, card or other material the design will be reproduced; whether you will be typing, handwriting, stencilling or using another method of producing letters; whether you will be including photographs or other types of illustration; and whether or not colour will be used.

These methods of producing lettering can be used in combination with one another: for example, a typewritten document could have a special heading made with transfer lettering. The amount of copy can provide an indication of the most appropriate method of production.

Handwriting

personal

However good your handwriting is, it is unlikely to be as attractive and well spaced as a specially trained calligraphic hand.

calligraphic hand

Typewriter

Manual typewriters tend to produce type of varying density

Typewriters are available with many different typefaces and type sizes. Manual typewriters do tend to produce type of

varying pressure because of the unevenness of key pressure, however.

Electric typewriters produce type of consistent density

On the other hand, electric typewriters produce type of constant blackness and some have the additional advantage of having the facility to adjust

the spacing between letters. All but the most sophisticated machines produce non-proportionately spaced type.

Stencils

home made

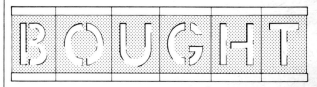

Stencils can be bought or made, but are really only suitable for larger size type. The distinctive character of

their letterforms has been exploited by professional designers to give a homely feel to a piece of design.

Dry transfer lettering

PRESSURE SENSITIVE

CUTOUT

With a little care, type of the highest quality can be produced with dry transfer lettering.

Typesetting

many different kinds of faces

Despite the large range of typefaces that are available, typesetters tend to have a relatively small selection. Always check what is available before you finalize your design.

WHAT IS MOST SUITABLE?

Typesetting is often the best letter generation method to use when you are producing a magazine, book or leaflet, for example, which includes more than 100 words of text. But sometimes other methods are more appropriate. Handwriting, dry transfers and hand lettering can be used for headings and small amounts of body type, while a typewriter is excellent for presenting straight-forward information with no frills. Also take into account how professional a result you want, and the relative cost of each method.

	handwriting	typewriter	stencil	dry transfer	typesetting
Less than 20 words eg. posters (headlines)	✓	✓	✓	✓	✓
20-100 words eg, posters, small ads, handbills	✓	✓			✓
100 or more words eg. leaflets, books, magazines (text)		✓			✓

Non-proportionately spaced type

You only need to study the letters of the alphabet to appreciate that their widths are different. Whereas 'n' and 'o' are about the same, 'm' is a good deal wider than 'i'. When type is produced so that each letter (or, in printer's terminology, *character*) is made to fill the same space it is said to be non-proportionately spaced. Most manual typewriters produce non-proportionately spaced type and the design of each character is carefully devised to reduce the effect of constant spacing. The 'i' is widened and the 'm' is squeezed up so that they and every other character fill the same space.

Handwriting

If you have a very low budget, hand-drawn lettering is a sensible way of getting your message across. The only cost is the pen, the ink and the paper. But, for it to be effective, only headings and small amounts of text should be handwritten; otherwise it will be difficult to read easily. If your handwriting is clear and consistent you could use it, although it is worth learning a style of 'calligraphic' handwriting which is excellent for a wide variety of jobs. (See opposite for different handwriting styles.)

All the examples below are written with a ball-point pen, which is not an easy instrument to use well. The drawing instruments that you can use to make lettering give various thickness of line and the inks can be watered down to give different shades. You can use different styles of handwriting, choosing the most appropriate style for your item. The flower show poster would suit an italic script, rather than an overpowering bold hand.

good handwriting

The factors which are characteristic of good handwriting are: consistency of style, well-formed characters, even spacing and alignment.

bad handwriting

Any handwriting which is at all difficult to read, and which therefore could confuse rather than inform, should not be used in any artwork.

WRITING IN CAPITALS

These too, if they are to work, must be evenly spaced and consistent. In any case, capitals should only be used for very small amounts of copy.

badly spaced writing

The reason this is unacceptable is that it will look extremely untidy and therefore will not attract the attention you intend it to.

DECORATIVE HANDWRITING

Flower

When writing words for display, try to make the letters large and eye-catching. A bold style is often the most effective.

writing Italics

One of the most attractive forms of handwriting is the italic style. Italic letters slope forward and are best written with a pen nib that can make thick and thin strokes.

Swash letters are a style of letter characterized by flourishes at the top and bottom of characters.

Decorative letters are usually used at the beginning of the text to show where the reading text starts.

writing script

Developed from the formal court and social writing of the 17th century, script imitates handwriting in a flowing, often slanted, style.

31

Stencils

Another hand-generated, non-proportionately spaced lettering system is the stencil – plastic or card strips out of which letter shapes have been cut.

The stencil below is typical of the sort obtainable from any good stationer or art supply shop. Stencils are used mainly for headlines or labels; stencilling more than a few words is time consuming and the result difficult to read.

The 'tea' and 'coffee' stencils were custom-made: a whole word cut out of card. The stencil was pressed against the fabric and an inked brush dragged across, leaving the words printed on the fabric. This is a quick labelling method.

Stencils can be used as a mask through which paint is sprayed or as a template for a letter. If you want to make a stencil, you can trace the stencil alphabet on page 110. Stencils have been made of maps, chemical symbols and numerous other signs and symbols. Their main advantage is that they can be used again and so can produce letterforms cheaply, and simple repetitive illustrations quickly. The disadvantage is that letter spacing with stencils is difficult and it is hard to avoid an amateurish look (see chapter 8).

Stencils are especially suitable when the type size needs to be large and quality is not important. The applications (right) shown are good examples. An added advantage is that the stencil can be used repeatedly.

Typewriters

There are two basic sorts of typewriters: the standard manual model and the more expensive electric typewriter.

The letters on the standard typewriter are all the same width. This gives the characteristic 'typed' look. If you draw lines down a page of typewritten text, you will see that each character (individual letter) occupies the same space.

The electric typewriter with interchangeable 'golfballs' has letters of different widths. Because the letters are spaced out more evenly, the copy looks better – you no longer get an 'm' squashed into the same space as an 'i'. The golfballs are available in different typefaces and type sizes, which allows you to change to *italic* or **bold,** or vary the type size whenever you want to. Electric golfball typewriters can be rented from print shops or office suppliers.

The letters on the standard typewriter

The spacing in a line of type produced by a manual typewriter is equal for each character. Typewriters are made with two standard spacings: ten characters per 2.5 cm (1 inch), called Elite; or 12 (Pica).

The letters on a non-standard typewriter

The type produced by some electric typewriters is proportionately spaced. And, since the typeface is not permanently fixed to the machine – it is carried on a golfball or 'daisy' wheel – it can be changed.

Typewriters are a versatile and cheap method of producing neat, readable type. If you use a high-quality electric typewriter, the results will be almost as good as this printed page. The major disadvantage is that the space between the lines is confined, usually to 6-point units or to *line spaces* (½-line, 1-line, 2-line and 3-line spaces). The ½-line space, which is normally only available on more expensive machines, is especially useful for separating a heading from the main text.

Typewriters have tabulator levers to align the copy on the left-hand side of the page, and to define the length of each line. Most machines also have a 'tab' key which makes the carriage jump across a set space, enabling you to indent paragraphs uniformly and to type columns easily.

If the type face on the typewriter is too large for your purposes, pages of typescript can be reduced with a photocopier or photographically.

Proportionately spaced type

When type is produced so that each character sits in a space which is proportionate to its natural width it is said to be proportionately spaced. Unlike ordinary typewriting, proportionately spaced type varies greatly in character width; the character 'i', for example, occupies very much less space than say 'm'. Each character can be designed to look pleasing without the need to fill a constant space. The type on this page is proportionately spaced. It is attractive to look at and easier to read than typewriting, but its varying character width makes it more difficult to handle.

Hot metal typesetting

All metal type is produced by pouring molten lead alloy into special moulds. Characters can be produced individually, or alternatively the moulds for a whole line of type can be arranged in the correct order and one piece (*slug*) made from

---

DIFFERENT KINDS OF TYPE

Each typeface usually has a series of different kinds and weights of type within it. The most common of these is Roman, or medium; this is what the text in this book is set in.

To emphasize something, italic (which has sloping letters) or bold (the same as medium but heavier) is used. These are all available in both upper and lower-case letters.

Lorem ipsum dolor sitamet, dignissum qui consectetur adipiscing elit, sed diam nomuny eiusmod tempor incidunt ut labore et dolore magna aliquam erat volupat
8/9 pt Century medium, ranged left to 17½ picas

Lorem ipsum dolor sitamet, dignissum qui consectetur adipiscing elit, sed diam nomuny eiusmod tempor incidunt ut labore et dolore magna aliquam erat volupat Ut enim ad
8/9 pt Century itals, ranged left to 17½ picas

Lorem ipsum dolor sitamet, dignissum qui consectetur adipiscing elit, sed diam nomuny eiusmod tempor incidunt ut labore et dolore magna
8/9 pt Century bold, ranged left to 17½ picas

---

them. Individually moulded type is more faithful to the original design but is slower to produce than line type. Small letterpress jobs are usually set from ready moulded type held by the printer. The type is arranged by the compositor in a device called a stick and then transferred to the printing machine. Larger jobs are set from freshly moulded type, each character being moulded as it appears in the copy.

Photosetting

Metal type is cumbersome and makes heavy demands on storage space. This and many other problems associated with hot metal setting were solved with the invention of photosetting. The photosetting system uses photographic images of each character through which light is passed. The light then projects the image on to photographic paper or film. Each character is projected in sequence so that each word and line is set in the correct position.

ART CENTER COLLEGE OF DESIGN LIBRARY
1700 LIDA STREET
PASADENA, CALIFORNIA 91103

Dry transfer lettering

The only proportionately spaced hand-generated letters, dry transfer lettering, looks like printed type. It works on the same principle as other transfers; that is, when you rub one side of a transfer, an image (*letterform*) sticks to any smooth surface.

The letters are bought in different typefaces and type sizes on plastic sheets with a protective backing paper. Each sheet has a series of spacing tabs which measures the correct distance between letters. A dry transfer catalogue shows the available sizes of the particular typeface, and is a useful reference source.

Detailed instructions on how to use dry transfer lettering are given in chapter 8.

Dry transfer lettering has a clean, professional appearance. The choice of typefaces is wide: both text and decorative typefaces, suitable for headings, are available and so are the Greek, Arabic, Cyrillic and Hebrew alphabets. The letters can be transferred on to paper, metal,

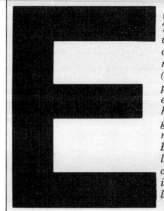

E

Typefaces available in the various dry transfer ranges can often be bought in a wide range of sizes. The small E (above) is equivalent to 6 point, while the large one (left) equals 192 point. Note that a height measurement is usually given in preference to the more normal type designation. Before you buy a sheet of lettering check in the catalogue (below) whether it includes both capitals and lower-case characters.

wood and plastic as long as the surface is smooth but not highly polished. They are available in colours and black and white: use light letters on a dark surface and vice versa. All these letters can be used as artwork, that is, for making an original which will be photocopied or printed (see chapter 9).

Dry transfer lettering works like any other transfer system. It is an easy way to give an item a professional finish, as it not only looks like printed type, but also has spacing tabs to help you space the letters correctly.

Type

Several terms are used frequently when talking about type.

The *baseline* is the line the type sits on. The capital letters are called *capitals* or *upper case* and the smaller letters are called *lower case*. The *x height* is the height of a letter 'x', which varies depending on the sizes you are dealing with.

How to measure type

Paper and distances on paper – such as the distance from the top of a page to the baseline of the first line of type–are measured in millimetres or inches. However, to measure type itself, and the spaces between type, smaller divisions are needed. In Britain and America a system called *picas* and *points* is used to measure type, while in Europe a slightly larger measure, the *Didot point,* is used.

The pica and point system dates back to when all type was produced in metal or wood. As the inch was the standard measurement in Britain and America, these countries based their type measuring system on divisions of the inch. (Europe had adopted the metric measurement system and naturally based its type measurement system on divisions of the metre.) The inch

The distance between the baseline and the top of an upper-case character is the cap (capital) height. However, in some typefaces several letters, such as L, are taller than the cap height.

The descender line is the lowest point any character will reach.

The distance between the baseline and the top of lower-case characters, such as a, e or x, is called the x height. The x height is a key feature of a typeface.

Metric measurements, especially millimetres, are useful to measure distances when producing artwork. They are easier to work with than fractions of an inch.

The pica and point system is based on the inch. If your ruler is marked in 1/12ths of an inch it can be read as picas (1 inch equals 6 picas).

was divided into six, each sixth of an inch was called a pica, and each pica was divided into 12 points. Since then, all type sizes and distances between characters and words have been measured in picas and points.

12 points = 1 pica
6 picas = 1 inch (2.5 cm)

so there are 72 points to the inch (2.5 cm).

These measurements are shown on a type scale, which is a ruler used to measure picas and points. The type scale often has a metric or imperial scale which is useful for measuring distances on paper. Type scales can be bought at graphic and art supply shops. (See page 38.)

Type was originally made by carving a single character out of wood. A character was either made directly out of a block of wood of a standard height, or made separately and fixed on to the end of a block. The characters were then arranged in the correct order, covered in ink and pressed on to paper, producing printed characters. This process, called *letterpress*, is still used today (see page 132), but now the letters are made in metal.

The illustration below shows a piece of metal type (made by pouring hot metal into a mould). The typeface is smaller than the type body that carried it: if a type size is called '12 point' this measurement refers to the body size.

HOW TYPEFACES DIFFER	
Rockwell	*The serifs in the Rockwell typeface are slab-like and as thick as the main body of the letter.*
Century	*Century is a classical serif typeface – one of the easiest of all to read – designed by L. B. Benton for the magazine* Century *(1881-1930).*
Nova	*Nova has a rounded but very short serif; the typeface is more suited to headings than body type.*
Univers Condensed	*Designed by Adrian Frutiger in 1957, Univers is available in a very flexible range of weights and dimensions; in this case, condensed.*
Helvetica Expanded	*As well as being condensed, a type form can be expanded. This example, in Helvetica, illustrates well how these faces are suitable for headings rather than text.*

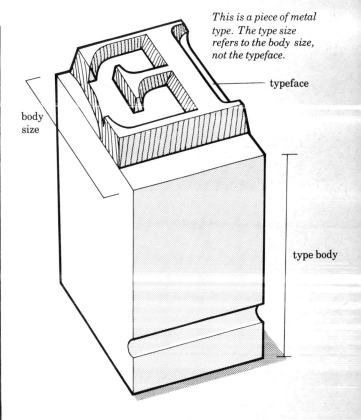

This is a piece of metal type. The type size refers to the body size, not the typeface.

typeface

body size

type body

USING A TYPESCALE

A typescale is designed to help you measure the number of lines of type that can be fitted into a space. If you know what type size you require (including leading) and the type area available, you can simply read off how many lines of copy you will need to fit a set number of lines of copy into the space. Alternatively, if you need to fit a set number of lines of copy into a given space, you can use the scale to establish what type size it must be set in. Trace off the scale on this page to make your own typescale – but remember it is unlikely to be completely accurate.

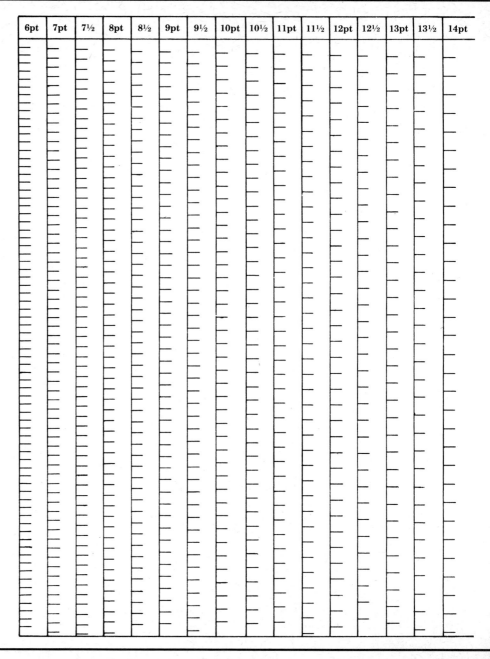

6pt	7pt	7½	8pt	8½	9pt	9½	10pt	10½	11pt	11½	12pt	12½	13pt	13½	14pt

The typescale can also be used to help with visualizing. Place the scale against the text area and mark off the base *lines for the appropriate type size. Then fill in the x height thickness with a pen or pencil. Remember that a type scale* *measures the distance between base lines, not the type size. If you want to use 8 point type* *with 2 point leading, mark off against the 10 point scale.*

The letterpress system of printing has now largely been superseded by photosetting, although it is still used today for quality work. But letterpress is the basis for virtually all terminology in typography. Photo-typesetting may be more up to date, but the vocabulary used for it has been in use for centuries. In the letterpress system, a line of type is set in a block, in a mirror image of what is to appear on the page (see above). To separate the words, pieces of lead are placed between them. As they are not as high as the letters, they do not print. See below for the sizes of leading available. In the line above you will note that the letter 'f' does not fit neatly on its block but is forced to hang over the end, while all other letters fit on to their alloted metal body.

The typeface is designed to allow it to fit alongside other lower-case characters, but great care would obviously have to be taken with leading if, say, a capital 'T' were to follow it.

The spacing available is based on divisions of the letter 'M'. The em-quad is the basic width and can be divided into 1 en (½ em), thick space (⅓ em), middle or mid space (¼ em), thin space (⅕ em) and hair space (⅙ em). Obviously the exact measurement of the 'M' can vary, depending on the face being used.

1 em quad

1 en

thick space

middle (mid) space

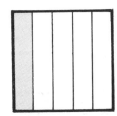

thin space

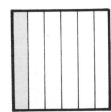

hair space

Word spacing

The way words are spaced in the letterpress system illustrates the spatial relationship between words and the type size: a small type size will have less space between the words than a large type size.

To make words and sentences using metal type, the characters are placed together in reverse order to form a line.

The words are separated from each other by *word spaces*, which are pieces of metal the same point size as the characters. The word spaces do not come into contact with the paper because they are not as high as the printing surface of the letters. With any typeface, the largest unit that could be used as a word space would be square; that is, for a 12-point typeface, a piece of metal 12 points wide and 12 points long. The other word spaces are divisions of this square – ½, ⅓, ¼, ⅕ and ⅙. The illustration (below, left) shows the spacing available when the type size is 72 point.

It is not necessary to give detailed instructions to a typesetter about word spacing unless you want very wide or narrow spacing.

Line spacing

The spaces between lines of type are called *leading*. Pieces of lead are used to separate lines of metal type, but they do not print as lines because, like the word spaces, they are not as high as the typeface. Line spacing does not alter the actual size of the typeface or lengthen the line; it simply moves the lines further apart. In the three examples of text setting below, one has no leading and is called *set solid*, and the other two have leading of different widths. In each case, the type size and typeface are the same.

The expression *8 on 9 point* means that 8-point type is being used with 1-point leading between the lines; the distance between one baseline and the next is 9 points. If the text is to be typeset 8 on 9 point with a heading in 10 point, it must be marked on the page of specifications that accompanies your job to the typesetters (see copy preparation, page 126). In the example it is assumed that the text is going to be 8 on 9 point and the heading is in 10 point. If you do not tell the typesetter that you want some extra space between the heading and the first line of text it will be set like this:

Heading
First line of type is too close because no extra space has been specified.

Heading
First line of type with extra space specified to provide white between heading and text

Both examples set in Cheltenham

When you want 2-point leading (space) under a heading that is 10 point, this should be expressed as 10 on 12 point. Alternatively, you can specify the type size of the heading (10 point) and instruct the printer to leave a 2-point line space beneath it.

LINE SPACING

Line spaces have several functions: they make the type on the page appear lighter (this is called *colour of type*; the more leading, the paler the type on the page looks); they make the text use up more space; they can be used as a means of arranging and grouping information; and they can affect legibility (that is, line spaces can make text either easier or harder to read).

Praesent luptatum delenit aigue duos dolor et qui molestias excepteur sint occaecat cupidatat non provident, semil. Tempor sunt in culpa qui officia deserunt mollit anim id est laborum et dolorfuga. Etharumd dereud facilis est er expedit distinct. Nam liber tempor cm et conscient to factor tum poen legum odioque civiuda. Et tamen in busdam
8/8 Garamond medium (set solid)

Praesent luptatum delenit aigue duos dolor et qui molestias excepteur sint occaecat cupidatat non provident, semil. Tempor sunt in culpa qui officia deserunt mollit anim id est laborum et dolorfuga. Etharumd dereud facilis est er expedit distinct. Nam liber tempor cm et conscient to factor tum poen legum odioque civiuda. Et tamen in busdam
8/10 Garamond medium (two point leaded)

Ranging Type

Careful manipulation of the spacing between words can produce a number of variations in the arrangement of lines of type. Hot metal and photographic systems of typesetting have the facility for producing columns of text made up of lines of equal length, known as justified setting. Alternatively type may be arranged so that only the left edge of each line is aligned vertically with the others. This type of setting is known as range left, ragged right. The arrangement can be reversed so that type aligns on the righthand side (range right, ragged left). All methods take up approximately the same amount of space; the important difference is one of appearance.

Lorem ipsum dolor sitamet, dignissum qui consectetur adipiscing elit, sed diam nomuny eiusmod tempor incidunt ut labore et dolore magna aliquam erat volupat Ut enim ad minim veniam, quis nostrud exerctation	Lorem ipsum dolor sitamet, dignissum qui consectetur adipiscing elit, sed diam nomuny eiusmod tempor incidunt ut labore et dolore magna aliquam erat volupat Ut enim ad minim veniam, quis nostrud exerctation	Lorem ipsum dolor sitamet, dignissum qui consectetur adipiscing elit, sed diam nomuny eiusmod tempor incidunt ut labore et dolore magna aliquam erat volupat Ut enim ad minim veniam, quis nostrud exerctation	Lorem ipsum dolor sitamet, dignissum qui consectetur adipiscing elit, sed diam nomuny eiusmod tempor incidunt ut labore et dolore magna aliquam erat volupat Ut enim ad minim veniam, quis nostrud exerctation
8/9 pt Garamond, ranged left to 9½ picas	8/9 pt Garamond, ranged right to 9½ picas	8/9 pt Garamond, centred to 9½ picas	8/9 pt Garamond, justified to 9½ picas

The Measure

The width of a line of type is called the measure, and it is measured in picas (that is, units of 12 points). The width of lines is always measured in 12-point units regardless of the type size. Below are three examples of text setting: each used the same type size, leading and typeface, but was set to different measures.

The wider the measure, the more characters fit into one line. For readability, a rough guide is to make the measure no wider than twice the type size in picas; in other words with 8-point type the maximum measure is 16 picas. To prevent the measure from being too narrow, go no less than your type size in picas; that is with 8-point type the measure should not be less than 8 picas.

Type can be arranged to fit any shape – for instance you may want to fill a circle with type or to take type up to the edge of an irregularly shaped illustration. Although this creates an interesting design it is sometimes difficult to read; but for small amounts of large copy (as in a poster) it can be very effective.

Lorem ipsum dolor sitamet, dignissum qui consectetur adipiscing elit, sed diam nomuny eiusmod tempor incidunt ut labore et dolore magna aliquam erat volupat Ut enim ad minim veniam, quis nostrud exerctation ullamcorpor suscipit laboris nisi ut. Traesent luptatum delenit aigue duos dolor et qui molestias exceptur sint occaecat cupidatat non provident, semil.

Lorem ipsum dolor sitamet, dignissum qui consectetur adipiscing elit, sed diam nomuny eiusmod tempor incidunt ut labore et dolore magna aliquam erat volupat Ut enim ad minim veniam, quis nostrud exerctation ullamcorpor suscipit laboris nisi ut.

Lorem ipsum dolor sitamet, dignissum qui consectetur adipiscing elit, sed diam nomuny eiusmod tempor incidunt ut labore et dolore magna aliquam erat volupat Ut enim ad minim veniam, ullamcorpor suscipit laboris nisi ut. Traesent luptatum delenit aigue duos dolor et qui molestias exceptur sint occaecat cupidatat non provident, semil. Tempor sunt in culpa qui officia

The three examples use type of the same size, but set to different measures. The most readable arrangement is above, which proves the general rule that the measure should be no narrower than the type size in picas and no wider than twice the type size.

This theatre programme includes three different arrangements of type. The cast names are in two columns, one ranged right, ragged left, and the other ranged left, ragged right. Underneath this is a block of justified type. The lines above these are centred on the page. The two blocks of type at the bottom are both ranged left, ragged right but centred on the overall text width.

On the Razzle

by Tom Stoppard *adapted from* Johann Nestroy

My purpose is to please, to entertain, to get people laughing . . .

JOHANN NESTROY

Weinberl	Peter Smith
Christopher	Catherine Kendal
Sonders	David Brown
Marie	Rosemary Hill
Zangler	Philip Brown
Gertrud	Naomi Schultz
A Foreigner	Jim Rissler
Melchior	Jack Rufus
Hupfer, the tailor	Lawrence Steinberg
Lightning	Andrew Burke
	Desmond String
Philippine	Sarah Jones
Madame Knorr	Charlotte Day
Frau Fischer	Christine Coole
Coachman	Lucien Knight
Italian Waiter	Gary Window
German Couple	Jack Daw
	Margaret Crans
Scottish Couple	Carlos White
	Brenda Snake
Second Waiter	Michael Cox
Constable	Anthony Mann
Fraulein Blumenblatt	Hilda Brent
Lisette, her maid	Victoria Spray
Ragamuffin	Hamish Rough

The name of Johann Nestroy is hardly known in Britain, but his work is not as unfamiliar as we may think. *On the Razzle* is the fourth re-working of Nestroy's *Einen Jux will er sich machen (He's Out for a Fling)*. The last time it was seen it went under the title of *Hello Dolly!*

The length of play is about 2½ hours which includes two 15 minute intervals.

This production is directed by Peter Dowle and assisted by Mary Tressle.

Character size (unit width)

The width of a particular character varies even within each typeface. The extended version of a popular typeface called Helvetica, for example, is considerably wider that the condensed version.

Unlike the standard typewriter characters, which all occupy the same space, each type character takes up a different number of units of a square.

The square is divided into 18 units, and word spaces, as well as the characters, are measured in these units.

Photo-typesetting, which is how nearly all type is now set, relies on this unit system, but simplifies it into 'wide', 'normal' or 'close' spacing.

Normal is a good choice for text setting. With headlines and display typefaces, which usually amount to just one or two lines of setting, you can choose from 'type touching' or 'close not touching' (the latter is generally better).

The character width of some typefaces appears to be identical; until a few words are set in each, it is not apparent that one is wider.

When a lot of text is set, these small differences can mean as much as one page more – or a page less – than you had planned for. So it is important to work out how the job will look and how many pages it will need using the exact typeface chosen. (See type samples on page 53 and copyfitting on pages 45-9.)

M M **M M** M M **M** M

A variety of characters exists within each typeface. Type can be light, medium and bold in weight, and condensed, normal and wide in width.

typewriting

In the standard typewriter typeface each character occupies the same space. With non-standard machines characters have different spacing.

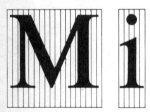

Unlike the standard typewriter characters which all occupy the same space, typeset characters each take up a different number of units of an em square. The square is divided into a total of 18 units; in the example above the M takes up all 18 units, while the lower case i only uses five.

Lorem ipsum dolor sitamet, dignissum qui consectetur adipiscing elit, sed diam nomuny eiusmod tempor incidunt ut labore et dolore

Lorem ipsum dolor sitamet, dignissum qui consectetur adipiscing elit, sed diam nomuny eiusmod tempor incidunt ut labore et dolore magna

How to space
How to space

Each typesetting house has its own standard inter-letter spacing, referred to as 'normal setting'. Some designers prefer to specify tighter letter spacing, and there are various ways to express this. This type was specified as 'close but not touching'.

Display or headline type has to be set more carefully if obvious aberrations of spacing are to be avoided. The first example shows normal spacing applied to display while the second example indicates the close-not-touching method of spacing.

COPYFITTING

Copyfitting is a method of estimating how many lines the copy will make in a particular typeface. This is called *casting off* and is necessary simply because the copy cannot be organized into lines, columns and pages without knowing how many lines of typesetting it will make.

How to copyfit

First count the characters in the copy following these simple steps:

1. Type the copy on a standard typewriter; this way all the characters will occupy the same width.

2. Draw a pencil line down the right-hand side of the copy, halfway between the shortest and longest lines (excluding paragraph ends). Make sure that the line is straight so that each line of copy to the left of the pencil line contains the same number of characters.

3. Count the characters in one line from the left margin up to the pencil line. The word spaces and punctuation marks count as one character each. If the pencil line cuts through a word space treat this space as a character.

4. Multiply the number of characters in each line by the number of lines on the page.

5. Count up all the characters on the right of the line, including the word spaces that separate the last word on each line from the one beginning the next.

6. Add the total number of characters on the left of the line (see step 4) to the number of characters on the right. This figure gives you the total number of characters in your copy.

If accuracy is really important, subtract the number of characters that fall short of the pencil line on the left. When there is a large number of manuscript pages, a quick character count can be made by stopping at step 4 and multiplying the number of characters on an average page by the number of pages. Or you could count the number of words in the same way, and multiply the total by six (the number of characters in an average word). The number of characters may be very high, but make a note of it and use it to roughly calculate the number of typeset lines it will make.

If the copy includes short headings leave these out of the character count and note them separately, unless they are part of the text and do not occupy a line of their own.

If you have not got a typewriter, count the number of characters in an average line of handwriting and multiply this figure by the total number of lines. This method is inaccurate and you would have to compensate by allowing more space than you estimate you will need, in order to ensure all the words will fit in. It would be better to rent a typewriter or pay someone to type out your copy.

Once you know the total number of characters, it is possible to work out how many lines of any typeface and size that the copy will make. The length of line (the measure) affects the number of characters in one line, so this has to be fixed. For example, the copy on page 48 has 1,342 characters. It will be set in 7 on 8 point Times New Roman (the name of a typeface) justified to a 14-pica measure. Since the amount of leading – in this case a 1-point space between the lines – does not alter the actual number of lines, initially we are concerned only with the type size and not the spacing.

To find out how many characters will fit into a line 14 picas long when the type is 7 point Times New Roman you can do either of the following:
1. Take a three-line sample of unjustified 7 point Times New Roman, measure 14 picas and count the number of characters, then divide the number by three to find the average number of characters per line.
2. Use a copyfitting table (see page 47), which lists the average number of characters per line in any specific typeface. (You can obtain copyfitting tables from a typesetter, printer or typesetting machine manufacturer.) Here is a part of the table for 7 point Times New Roman 327 'Monophoto':

7pt Times New Roman

Length of line (picas)	8	9	10	11	12	13	14	15	16
No. of characters	28	31	34	38	41	45	48	51	55

At 14 picas there are an average 48 characters in a line of 7 point Times. The total number of characters in the copy you need to typeset can be divided by the number of characters in one line; the resulting figure is the number of lines the copy will make.

$$\frac{\text{total number of characters in copy}}{\text{number of characters in one line}} = \frac{\text{number}}{\text{of lines}}$$

For example $\dfrac{1,342}{48} = 28$ lines

So the copy will make 28 lines of Times New Roman 7 point when the measure is 14 picas.

The elements that have to be decided in order for copyfitting to be done are the typeface, type size and measure (width of column/length of line).

If any of these elements is altered the number of characters in one line changes, so new calculations must be done. If, for example, the size of the type was changed from 7 to 12 point,

COPYFITTING TABLES

TIMES NEW ROMAN

Point Size	length of line (picas)											Point Size
	8	9	10	11	12	13	14	15	16	17	18	
7	28	31	34	38	41	45	48	51	55	58	61	7
8	26	29	32	35	39	42	45	48	51	54	58	8
9	24	27	29	32	35	38	41	44	47	50	53	9
10	22	24	27	30	32	35	38	40	43	46	48	10
11	20	23	25	28	30	33	35	38	40	43	45	11
12	18	20	22	24	27	29	31	33	35	37	40	12

UNIVERS MEDIUM AND UNIVERS MEDIUM ITALICS

Point Size	length of line (picas)											Point Size
	8	9	10	11	12	13	14	15	16	17	18	
7	28	31	35	38	42	45	49	52	56	59	63	7
8	25	28	31	34	35	40	44	47	50	53	56	8
9	22	25	27	30	33	36	38	41	44	46	49	9
10	20	22	25	27	30	32	35	37	39	42	44	10
11	18	21	23	25	27	30	32	34	36	39	41	11
12	17	19	21	23	25	27	29	31	33	35	37	12

TIMES NEW ROMAN ITALIC AND TIMES BOLD

Point Size	length of line (picas)											Point Size
	8	9	10	11	12	13	14	15	16	17	18	
7	29	32	36	39	43	46	50	53	57	60	64	7
8	27	30	33	37	40	43	46	50	53	56	59	8
9	25	28	31	34	37	40	43	46	49	52	55	9
10	23	25	28	31	34	37	39	42	45	48	50	10
11	21	24	26	29	32	34	37	39	42	45	47	11
12	18	21	23	25	27	30	32	34	36	39	41	12

UNIVERS BOLD

Point Size	length of line (picas)											Point Size
	8	9	10	11	12	13	14	15	16	17	18	
7	25	28	31	34	37	40	43	46	49	52	55	7
8	22	25	27	30	33	36	38	41	44	46	49	8
9	20	22	24	27	29	31	34	36	39	41	43	9
10	18	20	22	24	26	28	31	33	35	37	39	10
11	16	18	20	22	24	26	28	30	32	34	36	11
12	15	17	18	20	22	24	26	27	29	31	33	12

TIMES NEW ROMAN SEMI-BOLD

Point Size	length of line (picas)											Point Size
	8	9	10	11	12	13	14	15	16	17	18	
7	26	29	33	36	39	42	46	49	52	54	58	7
8	24	27	29	32	35	38	41	44	47	50	53	8
9	22	24	27	30	32	35	38	40	43	46	48	9
10	20	22	25	27	30	32	35	37	39	42	44	10
11	18	20	23	25	27	29	32	34	36	38	40	11
12	17	19	21	23	25	27	29	31	33	35	37	12

UNIVERS LIGHT

Point Size	length of line (picas)											Point Size
	8	9	10	11	12	13	14	15	16	17	18	
7	28	31	35	38	42	45	49	52	56	59	63	7
8	25	28	31	34	37	40	44	47	50	53	56	8
9	22	25	27	30	33	36	38	41	44	46	49	9
10	20	22	25	27	30	32	35	37	39	42	44	10
11	18	21	23	25	27	30	32	34	36	39	41	11
12	17	19	21	23	25	27	29	31	33	35	37	12

ABCDEFGHIJKLMNOPQRSTUVWXYZ&ÆŒ

ABCDEFGHIJKLMNOPQRSTUVWXYZÆŒ

abcdefghijklmnopqrstuvwxyzfiflffffiflæœ

ABCDEFGHIJKLMNOPQRSTUVWXYZ&ÆŒ

abcdefghijklmnopqrstuvwxyzfiflffffiflæœ

£1234567890.,:;!?''-()[]— *,.:;!?''£1234567890*

ABCDEFGHIJKLMNOPQRSTUVWXYZ&ÆŒ

ABCDEFGHIJKLMNOPQRSTUVWXYZ&ÆŒ

abcdefghijklmnopqrstuvwxyzæœ .,:;!?''-()[]—

ABCDEFGHIJKLMNOPQRSTUVWXYZ&ÆŒ

abcdefghijklmnopqrstuvwxyzæœ .,:;!?''-()[]

£1234567890 *£1234567890*

there would be only 31 characters in a line 14 picas long:

12pt Times New Roman

Length of line (picas)	8	9	10	11	12	13	14	15	16
No. of characters	18	20	22	24	27	29	31	33	35

The sum can be done again with this figure.

$$\frac{1,342}{31} = 43 \text{ (always round the number up if you are left with a few characters)}$$

So the copy would make 43 lines.

Copyfitting tables are based on justified setting, which allows for full lines of type. When copyfitting for unjustified setting, you must make some allowance for the uneven lengths of each line. As a rough guide, when setting in 8-11 point using any line length 18 picas and over, make copyfitting calculations based on the maximum line length but minus 2 picas. If the line is shorter than 18 picas, it will be difficult to get an accurate calculation in this way, because often only a few complete words will fit on to a line (you should not hyphenate words in unjustified setting). The only accurate way to copyfit unjustified setting is by tracing the characters from type sample sheets, but this is very time-consuming.

Copyfitting the headings
The headings may be in a different typeface or size, so copyfit these separately. The heading in the example on the right, 'The Main Heading', will be in 12 point Times semi bold (which is larger and darker than the 7-point text). It can be copyfitted in one of two ways:
1. Trace off the heading using a sample sheet of 12 point Times semi bold (see page 53) and measure how many lines it makes.

The Main Heading
This sample page of copy has been typed on a standard typewriter. All the characters occupy the same space, which is why you can draw a straight line down the page without cutting through a letter. If you find that you cannot draw a straight line down the page without cutting through a few letters this means your typewriter is not standard.

This paragraph is starting further into the page: this is called a 'paragraph indent'. You may want your paragraphs to start with an indent 1 pica wide; if so you should mention this in your specifications. Alternatively you may prefer a little space to separate the new paragraph from the old; if this is the case write down how much space you want. Measure with a typescale from the baseline of the last line in the old paragraph to the baseline of the first line in the new paragraph. You can then say, for example, that you want the first line of each new paragraph to be 8 on 12 point, assuming your typesize is 8 point and you want a 4 point space between paragraphs. A depth scale is a handy instrument for measuring spaces between lines, and you can buy one from any good art shop. With a depth scale you could easily measure lines of 14 point or 12 point, as the divisions marked are made for this purpose. Alternatively you could use the relevant scale in this book on page 38.

The Main Heading
This sample page of copy has been typed on a standard typewriter. All the characters occupy the same space, which is why you can draw a straight line down the page without cutting through a letter. If you find that you cannot draw a straight line down the page without cutting through a few letters this means your typewriter is not standard.

This paragraph is starting further into the page: this is called a 'paragraph indent'. You may

Above are two examples showing the difference between two type sizes.

Note the difference in the number of words in a line.

2. Count the characters in the heading – there are 16 in our example – and then consult the table for Times semi bold 12 point:

12pt Times semibold

Length of line (picas)	8	9	10	11	12	13	14	15	16
No. of characters	17	19	21	23	25	27	29	31	33

In the table we can see that 29 characters of 12 point Times semi bold will fit into a 14-pica measure so the heading will fit easily within that space and probably only take up about half of the line.

How much space the lines take
The copy in the example will use 28 lines of 7 point Times New Roman and one line of 12 point Times semi bold. It is at this stage you must take into account the fact that there are 1-point spaces between the lines – so the text will take up 28 lines of 8 point depth: 28 multiplied by 8 equals 224 points. The heading is another 12 points and you could add a 2-point space between the heading and the text. This makes a grand total of 238 points. When you get large numbers of points it is easier to convert them into picas and points by dividing by 12: 238 divided by 12 equals 19 picas plus 10 points.

This measurement allows you to do a very accurate rough visual.

Fitting the copy into less space
Changing the typeface is not a very effective way of saving space unless the original typeface was very expanded (wide). Lengthening the line, setting the text solid and reducing the type size are the most effective ways of saving space.

If the copy has already been typeset and there are too many lines, you have several options:

1. Get the copy reset but change the size or the line length.
2. Get the typesetting reduced photographically.
3. Delete some of the copy.
4. Reduce the margins at the top and bottom of the page to squeeze a few extra lines in. But beware of making the page look too crowded.
5. Use more paper. This is sometimes the cheapest and best thing to do, even though it may involve redesigning the pages.

Choosing a suitable typeface

The line of letter 'g's below, in different typefaces, shows how various are the ways of forming the same letter.

Although these are all the same type size, some appear smaller and some darker. Interestingly, each one of these typefaces was created at a different time and to a certain extent this has fashioned its look. They are shown in chronological order on page 50.

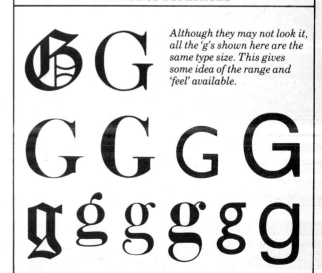

A RANGE OF TYPEFACES

Although they may not look it, all the 'g's shown here are the same type size. This gives some idea of the range and 'feel' available.

𝕲𝖔𝖙𝖍𝖎𝖈	15th century	**Black face**
Caslon	early 18th century	**Traditional 'Old' style**
Baskerville	late 18th century	**Transitional**
Bodoni	late 18th century	**Modern**
Gill	20th century	**Contemporary**
Helvetica	20th century	**Contemporary**

Gothic, which appeared in the fifteenth century, was derived from handwriting. However this face was not very legible and as printing developed other types emerged. Caslon, which also resembles writing, is finer and unlike Gothic is still used. Baskerville, which emerged soon after Caslon, has less serifs and is a transitional face coming between the old and new styles. The movement to more stylized type continued with Bodoni, regarded as the first modern style. Gill and Helvetica faces both lack serifs and were designed in the present century.

Before the invention of printing in the fifteenth century, whole books were painstakingly written out by monks and scribes, who used reed or quill pens.

The words in the last column of the table (above) describe the style of type (there are many typefaces that could be listed under each style). With the exception of the Gothic face, the ones shown in this example are all good text typefaces.

The difference between the Gothic typefaces and traditional typefaces, such as Caslon, is considerable. The Gothic typeface was designed to look like the script in handwritten manuscripts. Caslon also resembles handwriting, but the kind of writing which is executed with a reed or quill pen.

Letterforms moved towards a more stylized appearance with the invention of traditional faces such as Baskerville, which has the sharpness of an engraving. This movement away from handwriting continued through the modern faces that accentuated thick and thin strokes, and contemporary faces bear little or no resemblance to handwriting.

Gill and Helvetica, for example, are more geometric than the earlier faces; Gill looks more handcrafted as the thicknesses of the strokes do vary. This typeface was made by a stone mason, and reveals the influence of stone cutting and handwriting in the steady move away from the

ABC abc

Bembo serif

ABC abc

Rockwell slab serif

ABC abc

Bodoni hairline serif

ABC abc

Helvetica sans serif

The Bembo face, also called Old Face, uses sloping serifs and features little difference between the thin and thick slopes.

The Rockwell slab serif face is characterized by an even thickness of form that employs slab-like serifs. Its condensed forms are called Italian.

The Bodoni hairline face, which developed from Bembo, stresses the vertical strokes and features hairline thick serifs and cross-strokes.

The Helvetica sans-serif face lacks serifs altogether and is characterized by uniform thickness of stroke. It is widely used today.

hand-made towards uniformity. This is a natural progression, and the typefaces of today answer modern needs: Gothic would look out of place on a computer manual and Baskerville is too delicate for a motorway road sign.

The major difference between twentieth-century typefaces and earlier ones is the influence of the *sans serif* face. (*Serifs* are the small curves added to the ends of strokes: *sans serif* are typefaces without serifs.)

The sans serif typefaces look less fussy, almost clinical, and are used frequently in scientific or technical books, company reports and advertising because they lend a 'contemporary' look to the information. But serifs perform a useful function, in that they lead the eye into the letter and are generally thought to make reading more comfortable. So they are often used for text setting in books, magazines and newspapers.

Decorative typefaces

Decorative typefaces should not be used for text setting. They are more suitable for one or two lines of copy, as are 'display' or 'headline' typefaces.

Some typefaces are more decorative than

SOME DECORATIVE FACES

ABC	*Romantiques*
ABC	*Ringlet*
ABCD	*Shamrock*
ABC	*Shatter*
ABC	*Juliet*
ABC	*Futura Black*
ABC	*Egyptienne*

useful. It is important that you study type samples to ensure that you know exactly what the one you choose looks like and that you can obtain it locally. The Egyptienne bold condensed is called a *slab serif* face because the strokes end in blocks: this typeface could be used for a longer heading than Shatter, which is almost illegible. Choosing a decorative face is a matter of common sense.

Scripts
Script typefaces look very like handwriting, and they are often used to indicate quality or importance. It is not advisable to use scripts for more than a few lines of copy as they are tiring to read.

These examples of available scripts are based on different sorts of handwriting. The most popular is Palace script.

SOME SCRIPT FACES

Le Griffe · Aristocrat · Vivaldi · Squire · Park Avenue · El Greco · Commercial · Palace · Juliet · Bible Script · Balmoral · Brush Script

A font of type
A *font* of type is a collective term for all the available character shapes in a particular typeface. Below is a font of Times Roman (one of the few faces that has mathematical symbols).

ABCDEFGHIJKLMNOPQRSTUVWXYZ&
ABCDEFGHIJKLMNOPQRSTUVWXYZ*F*
abcdefghijklmnopqrstuvwxyz
£1234567890·*%[]!?--:;/(),.''©fflffififlffi
+×−±÷ √<>≃ ←~≃'''°≡…
† = △∞ ∥ ≃ ' '' °

A family of type
Each of the typefaces already mentioned – with the exception of the decorative faces – has variations based on the same letterforms that can be combined with it. For example, a line of Gill can contain Roman, italic or bold type all in the same family. Below are a few members of the Gill family:

Gill *Gill Italic*
Gill Light *Light Italic*
Gill Bold ***Italic***
Gill Extended

Some typefaces have larger families than others: Helvetica has over 15 alternatives. The head of the family is the upright form referred to as *Roman* or *medium,* and this and other versions, such as *bold* and *italic,* are available in all text typefaces.

Type samples

When you are trying to visualize how an item will look it is important to have good reference in the form of samples of different typefaces. Looking through a pile of samples can stimulate ideas and help you make decisions. Without reference you can make no decision as to which is the best typeface or size.

As you can see, each sample has a complete alphabet in Roman, bold and italic. The text setting gives you an idea of how the text will look in different typefaces. You can use these samples for tracing when visualizing.

ABCDEFGHIJKLMNOPQRSTUVWXYZ
abcdefghijklmnopqrstuvwxyz
ABCDEFGHIJKLMNOPQRSTUVWXYZ
abcdefghijklmnopqrstuvwxyz
ABCDEFGHIJKLMNOPQRSTUVWXYZ
abcdefghijklmnopqrstuvwxyz
$£1234567890.,:;!?''-()[]— *$£1234567890*

Lorem ipsum dolor sitamet, dignissum qui consectetur adipiscing elit, sed diam nomuny eiusmod tempor incidunt ut labore et dolore

10/11 point Times ranged left to 17½ picas.

ABCDEFGHIJKLMNOPQRSTUVWXYZ
abcdefghijklmnopqrstuvwxyz
ABCDEFGHIJKLMNOPQRSTUVWXYZ
abcdefghijklmnopqrstuvwxyz
ABCDEFGHIJKLMNOPQRSTUVWXYZ
abcdefghijklmnopqrstuvwxyz
$£1234567890.,:;!?''-()[]— *$£1234567890*

Lorem ipsum dolor sitamet, dignissum qui consectetur adipiscing elit, sed diam nomuny eiusmod tempor incidunt ut labore et dolore

10/11 point Univers ranged left to 17½ picas.

How to obtain samples

Books like this one contain samples of type. Your local library may have copies that you could photocopy.

Typesetters and *print shops* can usually give you samples of the typefaces they stock. These samples can be used for tracing, copyfitting and visualizing.

A *dry transfer lettering catalogue,* for example the Letraset catalogue, is a good reference for decorative and headline lettering. Catalogues can be bought from any good graphic or art suppliers.

Magazines and *newspapers* are worth keeping for picture and decorative typeface reference: for example, you could trace a word or cut out a heading to use on your own project. Cut out the items you want to keep and store them in a file grouped under subject areas so you can find them quickly when needed.

Tracing typefaces

In the copyfitting section, the importance of tracing characters to ensure that the headings fit into the available space was emphasized. Once you can see what the words look like in different typefaces and sizes you can see if there are any better alternatives. For the flower show programme, for example, you would trace out the words 'Flower Show' and the place in which the flower show is being held, 'Witcome and Bentham'.

A computer typeface would look completely inappropriate; on the other hand a seriffed face would look better.

The text that goes underneath the main heading can be represented by *tramlines* – lines that indicate the baseline and lower-case x height of the size of typeface you are using. If using 9 on 10 point Times Roman with a bold heading you need samples of both text and heading setting. From a sample of 9 on 10 point Times Roman, the x height can be marked on the edge of a piece of tracing paper.

Using a grid to position the columns (see chapter 7), draw lines 10 points apart to represent

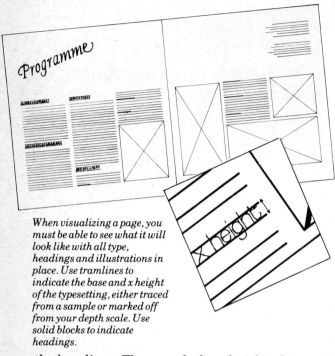

When visualizing a page, you must be able to see what it will look like with all type, headings and illustrations in place. Use tramlines to indicate the base and x height of the typesetting, either traced from a sample or marked off from your depth scale. Use solid blocks to indicate headings.

the baselines. Then mark the x height of 9 point Times Roman above each baseline.

Drawing in these lines gives an impression of how the type will look. Here it is shown with a sample of 9 on 10 point Times; and you can see that tramlines are a good way of representing lines of type.

Tracing the heading

To trace any heading you need a semi-transparent paper, such as tracing paper; the type sample; a hard pencil, for example a 4H; eraser; ruler; pencil sharpener, and a flat surface to work on. Keep the pencil very sharp and lean your drawing hand on a separate sheet of paper – not on the tracing paper, as the warmth of your hand can wrinkle the paper.

If you are unsure about the spacing, trace out different ways of dealing with the heading,

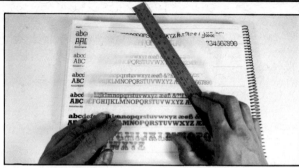

1. Place a piece of tracing paper over the type sample and draw lines on it along the baseline, x height and cap height of the type sample with the ruler and sharp pencil.

Turn over the tracing paper so that the pencil lines are on the back and can be rubbed off later without smudging the tracing.

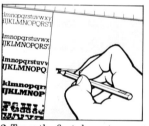

2. Trace the first character using the pencil guidelines to position the paper. Outline the letter first and then shade it in.

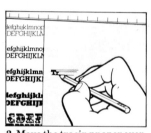

3. Move the tracing paper over the next character in your heading. Place it close to the first letter, but do not allow the letters to touch, and use the guidelines as before.

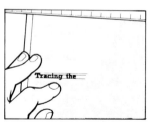

4. When you come to a word space use the width of the letter 'i' as the space you leave; this can be marked off before commencing the next word.

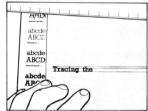

5. If you need another line of heading underneath, you can get an idea of how much space you need between the lines by placing your tracing over the type sample and moving it about until you are happy with the spacing.

varying the spacing each time until you find the one that you prefer. If pictures are to be included you can represent these with either a rough sketch or a box.

Rules and borders

Rules, or straight lines, come in various thicknesses and are measured in points or ½ points or in 'fine', 'medium' and 'thick'.

If you want rules you have to specify to the typesetter what thickness, what length, and where the rule is to go (see copy preparation, page 126).

Rules have the following functions:
1. To separate categories of information; for example, numbers and words.
2. To draw attention to information; by underlining, for instance.
3. To link information, such as words and numbers.
4. To decorate.

Although horizontal rules are treated as type, vertical rules usually add to the typesetting costs. Find out how much they will cost, and if they are too expensive you can draw the lines in by hand. Different ways of making straight lines are shown on page 113.

If you want a rule to appear in the text – for example under headings – make it the length of the measure (line width). Rules are best used sparingly; leaving a space between lines is often a better way of separating information than putting in lines.

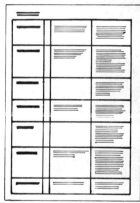

These two examples show what to do and what not to do. Vertical lines not only look unattractive, but are also *expensive to set. It is far better to use the blocks of type and spacing to create vertical lines. Try to use all rules sparingly.*

Borders are largely decorative. Typesetters do not usually have much of a selection so it is best to put them in by hand (see how to use dry transfers on page 107).

Borders are used mainly on invitations and items with a nostalgic or traditional air. It would be appropriate in the flower show example mentioned at the beginning of this chapter to use a decorative border. Like rules, they look best when used sparingly.

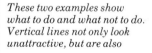

RULES AND BORDERS

A border need not be just a plain black rule, as the examples here show. They can easily be traced or copied from a book.

Pictures

A picture will either attract or inform, or both. Do you need a picture to attract attention? This is often the case with posters and display items, but pictures in books and leaflets which are decorative are often attracting attention as well. Do you need a picture that informs? The informative picture shows how something is done or what a particular object looks like, or records an event. The following questions are useful in identifying whether a picture is needed and what kind it should be:

1. Do you need to attract attention to your message with pictures or are words adequate?

2. Is there part of the text that is unclear and could be explained by a picture?

3. Is there something constantly referred to in the text – for example a place, person or event – that could be illustrated to help the audience relate to what is being said?

4. Is there a sequence of events, such as a step-by-step process, that could be illustrated to help the reader understand what is going on?

5. Is there a mood or style that could be captured by a picture or an appropriate symbol?

6. Would the audience you are aiming at prefer to have the text broken up by pictures to provide light relief from continous reading?

Types of picture
Different types of pictures can perform the same function; for example, a photograph can show what a place looks like and so can an illustration.

The degree to which you want to inform or attract can help you select a particular sort of picture.

Functions of pictures
1. *To explain instructions.*
The diagram is the most commonly used for this function: it can be used to show unrealistic views, such as a cross section through an object, or a complicated molecular structure. Because a diagram is made to perform a specific function, it is not cluttered with unwanted information. This usually makes diagrams clearer than photographs or illustrations.

2. *To attract attention.*
The diagram does not usually grab the attention in the way that a photograph or drawn illustration can. The type of picture you choose depends to a large extent on the type of audience you are aiming at. For example, a craftsman advertising his skills might find a drawn or painted illustration more in keeping with his hand-made tradition than a photograph. Obviously colour attracts attention, but it is not the only means of doing so. Simple, one-colour items can be just as effective.

3. *To explain concepts.*
Diagrams are often an excellent method of illuminating ideas; photographs are usually too realistic.

4. *To inform the audience of the appearance of a place, person or event.*
The degree of realism needed in this category defines the sort of picture used. An artist's impression of a place often bears little resem-blance to the actual place and instead conveys its mood and atmosphere rather than the factual position of houses and streets; on the other hand, diagrams such as maps can show its geographical features and layout without capturing the mood or style. Photographs will present a more rounded, but limited, view. Illustrations can draw attention to particular features that you may want to show, whereas photographs often

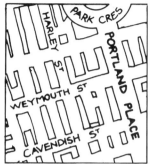

Sunflower

Sunflower seed

The map (left, top row) is a good example of an illustration used purely to convey information; it contains no additions to distract the attention.

The line drawing in the middle is another good example of an informative illustration.

The photograph of the Eiffel Tower is the only illustration to show exactly what its subject looks like.

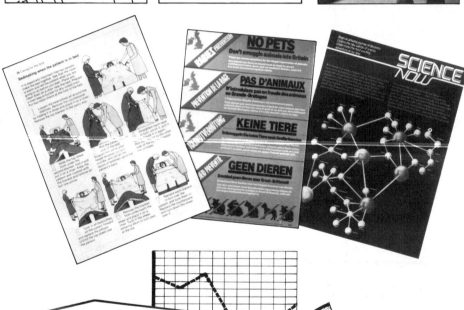

The illustrations on the left (middle row) clearly demonstrate a complicated sequence of events. Photographs could include extraneous material which would detract from the information being conveyed. The eye-catching design of the rabies poster (middle) attracts the attention of passers-by and at the same time imparts the sense of the danger associated with the subject. The third picture shows how a complicated molecular structure can be represented in one simple illustration.

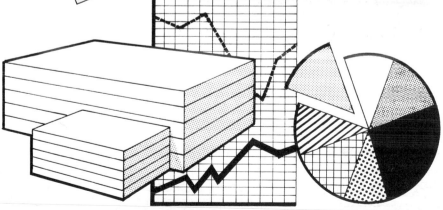

All three diagrams (bottom row) are ways of explaining complicated facts and figures in a way that can be understood at a glance. Each one is best at showing a particular sort of information. Trying to explain the annual sales figures, for example, by way of the pie chart would lead to total confusion.

Case history: illustrated publicity material for an hotel

An hotel owner wants to attract people to her hotel, explain the facilities of the hotel and list the prices. She wants to attract more than inform, so the illustrations she uses must make the most of whatever she has to offer.

A picture of the hotel on the cover of a pocket-sized leaflet would be a good idea if it is an attractive building; if not, then some aspect of the town could be shown instead, or a holiday atmosphere could be conveyed with the use of a symbol such as the sun.

Inside the leaflet the price list could be done with small symbols and numbers or, more simply, be arranged into a table.

The facilities – the cocktail lounge and steam room for example – could be shown by drawn illustrations, photographs or symbols. A picture of people sitting around in the steam room, looking happy and relaxed, would be preferable to a picture of a door with steam coming out of it. If the hotel is outstanding because of its authentic eighteenth-century atmosphere, it would be wise to use photographs. If it has only rather ordinary modern decor and furnishings, a combination of photographs and illustrations will liven up the leaflet and distract attention from the shortcomings of the hotel.

Obviously, a badly taken photograph – for instance, one which is grey and out of focus – does more harm than good. If the photographs have a bluish tinge, this could give the hotel a cold, unwelcoming appearance. A good photograph of an empty room might give the impression that the hotel is not popular. And a group picture of the 'cheerful relaxed staff' all standing rigidly to attention like grim-faced soldiers will not induce many people to come to the hotel.

All these factors alter the effectiveness of a message.

include what you do not want along with everything else. But when it comes to recording events – for example, the victorious tennis player leaping over the net, or the child victims of an earthquake – the photographer triumphs.

5. *To illustrate statistical information.*
Diagrams are the most commonly used form of picture when the subject is statistics. There are several methods of representing relationships between groups and numbers; see p.57 for a few examples. The important thing is that the diagram can be understood – all the elements in it must be clearly labelled, for example. One way of checking this is to get someone to interpret it after it has been finished: missing details which at first may have seemed too obvious to include might need to be added.

Photographs
Whereas a diagram or illustration is usually commissioned and drawn for a specific purpose, photographs are often chosen from an existing stock or library and may not, therefore, be precisely what you require.

Things to look out for when selecting a photograph are:

The content: what to leave out
If you have a picture with a lot of unwanted information then either exclude it or crop it (that is, print only a detail from it). Pictures can be improved with judicious cropping: it is common practice in newspapers, where pictures are cropped savagely to fit a space or to emphasize a relevant part of the picture. Unwanted information should be cropped from a photograph: for instance, a picture might look old-fashioned just because it includes an old car or people wearing clothes which are 30 years out of date. Use 'L shapes' (pieces of L-shaped card) to decide how the picture will be cropped (if at all). Move the L shapes around until you obtain the

Experiment with L-shaped pieces of card to discover which areas can successfully be cropped from a photograph.

best effect. Do not cut a picture; instead put a sheet of tracing paper over the top and mark the cropping lines on that.

The people in a picture
If people are included in the photograph look very

Although these photographs both show an adult and child, the expressions and positions convey very different moods and messages.

closely for any unwanted information. Postures, clothes, facial expressions and age can convey different impressions and moods. Look, for example, at the two pictures at the bottom of the previous page. Both are of an adult and child, but there the similarity ends.

The background

The background should be considered as well as the foreground. An hotel owner taking a publicity photograph of his or her hotel would make sure the garbage cans were removed and it was a bright day. If the background was unattractive it would be best to take a close-up of the hotel and exclude the background.

The focus

Are the edges crisp or fuzzy looking? There should be some point on every photograph – usually the subject – which is sharp and in focus. If the picture is badly focused, then do not use it. Printing will not improve a poor photograph.

Commissioning illustrations and photographs

When commissioning illustrations and photographs it is important to see a number of people's work, and then to choose one who has a style and interpretation which will be sympathetic to your subject matter.

Illustrations

If the illustration you are commissioning is an *informative* one it is essential that the illustrator is supplied with accurate reference from which to work, and that all aspects and requirements are explained clearly in a written brief. Ask the illustrator to produce an initial sketch so that you can check for accuracy. It is quite normal to make changes at this stage and they are not difficult to execute. Alterations made to the final drawing can be time-consuming, and expensive.

For an emotive illustration – one that creates an atmosphere – the style and approach of the illustrator is extremely important. In this case, the appearance and mood of the illustration is the crucial factor, rather than the information it might convey. Always discuss ideas with the illustrator, and be open to any suggestions he or she may make. If the illustration is to accompany an article, give it to the illustrator to read, along with any relevant visual reference.

For all illustrations, it is essential that the illustrator knows how the printer expects to receive the work. You must discuss this with the printer and finalize it before the illustration is commissioned.

Photographs

Although you should have a clear idea of the content and style of the image that you require you should again be open-minded to suggestions from the photographer which may improve your original concept. It is often helpful to draw out your ideas when discussing them – there may be technical difficulties which you had not foreseen. In studio work almost any effect can be achieved, but the more complicated the technical arrangements, the more time-consuming and therefore the more expensive the photograph becomes. In some cases you may wish to be present at the shoot to ensure that everything is carried out as you intended, but sometimes – at a portrait session, for example – you could inhibit the rapport the photographer must build up with the subject. Wherever possible, ask to see a polaroid of a colour photograph before the photographer takes the final shot. As with initial sketches for an illustration, changes made at this stage will incur minimal extra expenditure.

Always explain to the photographer as clearly as possible what effects you do want and what you do not want, and ensure that he or she clearly understands your intention.

5. DESIGNING STATIONERY

It is often said that the art of letter writing has declined, and for this the telephone is blamed. In fact, the volume of letters has increased steadily over the years. Despite modern communications systems, there still seem to be literally millions of reasons for people to put pen to paper.

It is usually much easier to be clear and precise when writing than it is when speaking on the telephone. Words can be changed; you can search for the right phrases, and polish what you have written. Sometimes the purpose of a letter is simply to make a permanent record of ideas, feelings or proposals. In business this can be extremely important, but personal thoughts too are often committed to paper rather than expressed in a face-to-face situation.

It is often important to create the right impression with a letter. A note to a close friend may only need to be legible and coherent. It is a different matter, however, if you are sending a letter to your bank manager requesting a loan, to a company about work you are doing for them, or simply to someone that does not know you well.

Writing the letter in your best handwriting, or typing it on good quality paper, will give the impression that you did it with some care. But printed note paper can create all kinds of impressions over and above the basic, well written, carefully presented letter.

Printed stationery is now inexpensive and easy to produce in small quantities: 100 sheets of good quality note paper can be bought and printed for as little as three times the cost of the blank paper.

Creating the right impression

These two examples of company letterheads use roughly the same layouts and have basically the same amount of information. Yet the impressions they create are distinctly different.

The one on the left looks very modern, giving the impression of a go-ahead company operating in the sphere of high technology. This has been achieved by using a computer typeface, lively colours and a well organised layout.

The one next to it uses a traditional script that suits the name 'Flowers' very well. It creates just the kind of approachable, classy impression that a high-quality restaurant would desire.

If the two businesses were to exchange their letterheads, you would see how inappropriate they become: the high-class restaurant appears

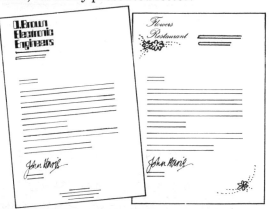

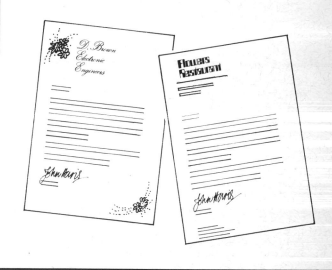

as perhaps a go-ahead snack-bar, while the identity of the electronic company is completely confused.

The typeface, colour and size have a great deal of potency and, consequently, must be carefully related to the image you wish to convey. Paper colours and qualities also add to the overall impression. White, with its simple neutrality, is the traditional, 'anonymous', colour for paper. Tinted papers can be restrained, cool colours such as grey or blue, while others, cream for example, are warmer. You can use typeforms which are printed in any number of colours on different coloured papers. In addition, there are numerous thicknesses and different textures and surfaces of paper, as well as colours, to choose from.

You must decide what you want to 'say' about yourself or your organization. Do you wish to create an intimate impression, a traditional one, or a businesslike one; say something about what you do; appear to be fashionable, humorous, caring or competent?

Your reaction to the previous examples, or to any piece of graphic design for that matter, is dependent on an already learned set of values about the letterforms used, the colours, and certain kinds of layout. Even without any formal training, most people have learnt a large amount about design and have opinions about it simply because they have seen literally thousands of examples. To find the right visual style for the impression you want to create, look critically at some of the examples showing use of type, colour and layout that you come across in the course of an ordinary day, and choose those examples which seem to have the qualities you are looking for. Make a check-list of the qualities these examples convey to you. Then compare those qualities with the ones which would most aptly represent you.

Study examples of letter headings to discover how they have been conceived and produced, and use what you learn to help you design your own.

Printing processes

You must decide at the outset how your stationery will be printed: some printing processes might suggest ideas you might not otherwise have had.

There are two printing processes which can be used to produce most of the stationery that you

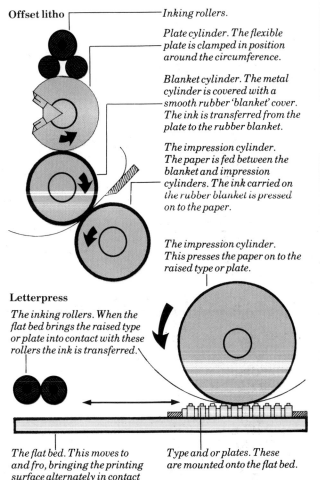

Offset litho

Inking rollers.

Plate cylinder. The flexible plate is clamped in position around the circumference.

Blanket cylinder. The metal cylinder is covered with a smooth rubber 'blanket' cover. The ink is transferred from the plate to the rubber blanket.

The impression cylinder. The paper is fed between the blanket and impression cylinders. The ink carried on the rubber blanket is pressed on to the paper.

The impression cylinder. This presses the paper on to the raised type or plate.

Letterpress

The inking rollers. When the flat bed brings the raised type or plate into contact with these rollers the ink is transferred.

The flat bed. This moves to and fro, bringing the printing surface alternately in contact with the impression cylinder and the inking rollers.

Type and or plates. These are mounted onto the flat bed.

POINTS TO CONSIDER WHEN CHOOSING:

LETTERPRESS
Pros
Jobs comprising small amounts of type in standard typefaces are quicker to organise than by lithography. If you want to adjust spacing or change type between jobs or after proofing then letterpress is cheaper as new plates do not have to be made.
Letterpress machines can usually handle heavier board than lithographic machines, and can crease and cut at the same time.

Cons
Letterpress printers are less common today and the home kits are limited for size. Also the type in the kits is quite difficult to handle.
Illustrations have to be printed from blocks which are expensive to make.
Letterpress printers usually typeset from their own range of type but the range available may be limited.
Assembling type with rules, borders and illustrations is more complex than it is with lithography. You will have to pay the printer to do it and give him specific instructions.

LITHOGRAPHY
Pros
Nearly every instant print shop has a small lithographic printing machine so access to them is usually easy.
Illustrations are easily handled by the lithographic process. If they are to be printed line they are treated in the same way as typematter.
You can use your own time and skill to put together the artwork used by the lithographic printer. The more complex the design the more work you are handling yourself.

Cons
Once the lithographic plate is made there is little that can be done to make changes without remaking it. Deletions are possible, but not rearrangement of material.
If you want to change the image between jobs new plates will have to be made, although for short run jobs the cheaper paper or plastic plates can be used.
There are a few types of material that the lithographic process cannot print on. If you want to use heavy or metallic board, discuss the problem with your lithographic printer beforehand.

are likely to need: letterpress and offset litho. The major difference between the two is in the preparation rather than in the finished work.

Good letterpress printing is of a very high quality, and the precision and definition of the characters is still unsurpassed. If your intention is to produce stationery in a standard typeface then it is an extremely satisfactory method. The printer composes the type, but you must present him or her with a clear specification of what you require (see page 126). By doing this you avoid having to produce artwork. Letterpress is not the most common printing method used these days, however, and it can be difficult finding an appropriate printer.

Most print shops and small printers use offset litho as their main printing process. The advantages are quite simple: the bulky cases of metal type and the tedium of hand composition have been replaced by a photographic process. The printer works from artwork which is photographed and the image is transferred on to a printing plate by a very quick and inexpensive process.

For this process you produce the artwork, although many printers do provide a design service. If you use this service, ask to see the artwork before it is printed to check if the type is crooked or words are misspelt, and so on. If you supply the artwork, it is your responsibility to ensure that it is correct (see pages 120-7 for preparation of artwork).

There are other specialized processes which are useful for stationery design. A process called thermography uses heat to produce a raised shiny effect on the inked areas. With embossing a pattern is pressed on to the paper.

A range of stationery

The most useful item of printed stationery is note paper. A standard sheet of note paper can be adapted for most of your stationery needs: it can be used for an invoice or statement, and for formal and informal letters. If you are working on a limited budget or are unsure of your design, it is best to print only a small quantity of note paper to begin with.

There are several other stationery items which might be useful, such as a printed invoice, a compliment slip, a business card, and perhaps a postcard.

Some simple conventions exist relating to

The letter- or note-paper size is either 210 × 297 mm, or 8½ × 11 inches; it can be folded twice across its width to fit a standard business envelope.

Corporation Street, Preston PR1 2TQ
Telephone: 0772. 51831

Embossing is another printing process suitable for stationery. A relief is pressed into the paper, and can be either inked or uninked, in which case it is called blind embossing. Blind embossing relies for visibility on the shadows around the raised letter.

LETTERHEAD

the relative sizes of each of these stationery items and the kind of information that they should carry.

If you keep to this commonly used system, there will be no paper wastage and you will get the maximum value for money. Other paper sizes and systems often require more complicated folding in order to fit envelopes or a standard filing system.

The standard business envelope is available in two alternative forms: with and without an address window, each of which has its uses.

If you have a large volume of letters, addressing the envelopes can be very time consuming, so then the window envelope is ideal. But the address must be positioned carefully on the original letter, and this should be taken into account when you are designing your note paper.

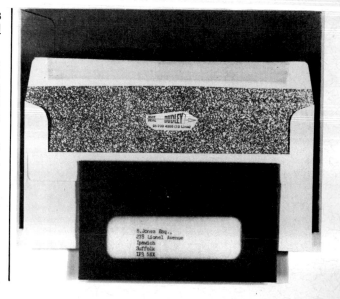

Smaller note paper for invoices and memos is usually two-thirds the size of letter paper. This can be folded in half across its width to fit the standard business envelope. If you need an invoice where you can detail 20 or so items, use letter-size paper.

Print the smaller size invoice or memo paper on letter-size paper and use the bottom of the sheet for compliment slips (usually one-third of the page) – the cost of this extra item will be a minimal cutting fee. Compliment slips fit the standard business envelope without folding.

Business cards vary enormously in size. The most useful basic format is about the size of a credit card, and fits conveniently into a wallet.

INVOICE FORM

COMPLIMENTS SLIP

BUSINESS CARD

BUSINESS CARD

BUSINESS CARD

Note paper

Letter-size paper is the central stationery item in any range: it is the most widely used, and from it the style and layout of all the other stationery items are usually derived.

For informal note paper, which is intended for handwritten letters and chatty notes to friends, the general layout and style of your note paper can be as elegant or humorous as you wish.

For instance, use a simple box to enclose the writing area and draw a small illustration or design, which is personal and light hearted, in the space above it. But keep it simple and uncluttered. Choose paper which is your favourite colour, and for the illustration use a symbol which is easily identifiable with you – if you are a keen gardener, for instance, a clump of plants or a gardening tool. Or design a classical heading for your writing paper.

Business note paper design, on the other hand, should be relatively conventional, for good reasons. Its function is to explain from whom and from where it has been sent (which is printed), and to whom (information which must be typed on to each letter). It should include any reference information which might be required by law, plus any other useful information.

The name and address of the sender is usually printed at the very top of the page, with any reference material – telephone and telex numbers, for instance – underneath. Information such as company directors or affiliated organizations are normally in a smaller type size at the bottom of the paper. Even if you do adhere to this basic order, there are many different ways in which to organize these various elements.

The typewriter grid

Since business or formal letters are usually typed, note paper designs should be related to the way in which a typewriter functions.

The standard typewriter operates on a very simple grid system, with each letter or number occupying the same amount of space.

The most commonly used margins are either 2.5-cm (1-inch) or 4-cm (1½-inches) inset from the start of the carriage, and all other stops for tabulation are at 1-cm (½-inch) or 2.5-cm (1-inch) intervals. The lines of typing are set 1 pica apart and can be increased by ½-line increments. So initially you can draw a simple grid pattern on to your letter-size paper, which will describe where the typing will start and how the words will be distributed across the page.

This grid should be used to position the information to be printed, so that typed letters will be visually consistent with the letterhead.

Of course, there are variations of spacing and line disposition on some typewriters; the grid should relate to the typewriter that you are going to use on your stationery.

With well designed letter headings, the position of the name and address and the other printed information makes sense in relation to the *typed letter,* not simply to the sheet of paper. This sort of guidance for typing is similar to the ruled lines and margins in school exercise books, which helped you write at a consistent size and in straight lines.

Experiment with ideas for letterhead designs. Letters and words do not need to be upright or even complete, and a background pattern can be used to high-light the text area.

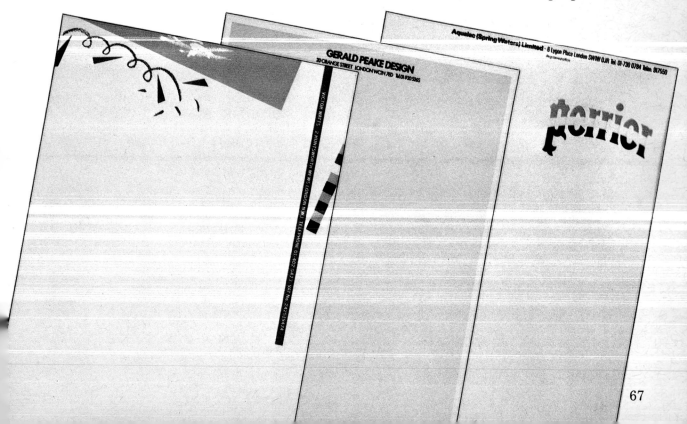

Designing a letterhead

Contact a printer or paper mill before you start your design to obtain paper samples: the kind of paper available will influence what typeface you use and other design decisions. Remember that the paper on which the finished artwork is printed is an important element of the design.

If you want to use a paper which is not obtainable from your printers, check that the paper you have chosen will be suitable for the printing process that will be used. With certain ranges of papers you can also obtain matching envelopes either with or without a window.

It is a common mistake to choose a typeface and size for the name and address which is too large: a letterhead should not assume the quality of a newspaper banner headline.

Draw your grid with light blue pencil on sheets of letter-size paper; experiment with different typefaces and layouts. Trace in the letters from a dry transfer lettering catalogue (see page 53) and then fill them in with black or coloured pens. Once you are satisfied with a design, photocopy it on to the paper it will be printed on, then type a letter on the photocopied sheet: this will show you exactly what the finished note paper will look like. (It is also a good idea to photocopy the design again twice: cut one-third off the bottom of one sheet, and two-thirds off the bottom of the other, to check whether the heading works on an invoice and a compliment slip.) If you have a symbol or logo, it should be incorporated into your stationery design.

The name (with the logo or symbol) is, of course, the central part of the whole composition, so try to feature it in some way. You could make it larger and use a distinctive typeface. You could use a second colour to separate it out from the other information as in these examples.

Try to limit the size for the address and telephone number (and any other words, such as 'date', 'our reference', and 'your reference') to 12 point or smaller. You will rarely need to make these elements larger. If the name is in a simple undecorative style, try using a lighter or bolder version of the same typeface.

Set out the address in several different ways, either in short lines as a block, or strung out in a single line, perhaps underlining the name. The examples in this chapter can either be copied or used as a starting point from which you can develop your own ideas.

Invoices

Whether you have used an illustration, symbol or simple typographic design for your letterhead, that decision will have some bearing on the other items in the stationery range you produce.

The invoice contains more information than the other pieces of stationery, and is the most complicated item you will have to design. It must be organized into space for descriptions, costs and a total cost. It might also include terms of payment: 'payment to be made within 30 days of the date of invoice', for example.

In Britain, if the invoice is sent by a registered company, there are certain legal requirements which must be met. For instance, the registered office and number of the company, the registered VAT number, the date, and the word 'invoice' must all appear, and the actual amount of VAT must be shown separately from the total.

The invoice should display all the required information, plus the recipient's account details, in an order which is both clear and logical but which also retains the overall impression that you have created with your letterheaded note paper. The symbol and name, and the information which is common to both the letter paper and the invoice, should remain in the same place at the same size. Any extra information should be incorporated into the typewriter grid. Additional reference material should appear at the top, in the same area as on the note paper. The word 'invoice' must be relatively prominent, but not so that it detracts from the name of the sender. It is often placed just above the area which contains the description of the work, service provided, or items being charged for.

It is important to refer to the typewriter grid again when designing the areas for description of services or goods and the costs. Use the tabulator stops on your typewriter when deciding where the columns will go. The cost column must be wide enough to include the currency symbol and

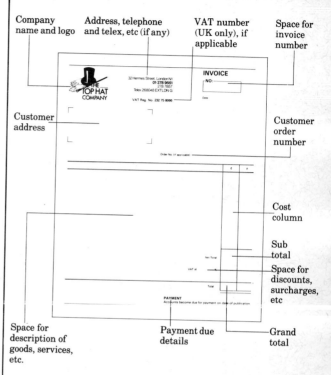

perhaps six or seven numerals. Conventionally, the text area is divided so that the description starts at the left-hand margin, while the costing columns are on the right-hand side of the typing area, as shown in the example above.

At the bottom of the invoice, provide a space for the total cost.

Generally, it is better to design a more flexible layout, using single vertical lines to make columns, so that when the typing is not quite correctly positioned it does not detract from the overall impression of organization and neatness.

Any subsidiary information, such as a statement relating to the terms of payment, is arranged at the bottom of the paper outside the typing area.

The compliment slip

This is a document which usually accompanies goods or information the recipient is expecting because of some prior arrangement. The slip can have a short message written on it or just a signature, or it can even be sent blank.

You can simply repeat the note paper design on the compliment slip. It is not necessary to include the subsidiary information such as directors or registered office, since this is a relatively informal communication.

The only new information to include is the the words, 'with compliments'.

If you separate these words out from the rest of the copy, as is the usual practice, they are

In this example the postcard, compliment slip and business card all have the same logo, thus reinforcing the company identity and image.

Their varying sizes reflect the separate functions and the amount of information that each form of stationery is intended to convey.

isolated in a relatively large area. This is enough to highlight them. It is not necessary to make them very large; once again, restraint will often create a greater impact.

The postcard

This is another very useful item of stationery, which can serve the same purpose as a compliment slip, but which has the added advantage that it does not need an envelope. Plain cards can be bought cheaply from any stationers or printer, and then printed with either existing letterhead artwork (which will probably need to be reduced photographically, sometimes called *photomechanical transfer*, or *PMT*), or with new setting. Because of the limited space, the sender's name and address are usually arranged in one line along the top of one side of the postcard.

Business cards

The purpose of the business card is to eliminate the hurried and awkward scribbling of your name, address and telephone number on to a scrap of paper or back of a cigarette pack for somebody that needs it.

The card usually includes your name (and, if appropriate, that of the company or organization you represent), address and telephone number and, possibly, your position in the company or organization. It is usually small enough to fit into a wallet and is therefore usually about credit-card size.

Because business cards are so much smaller than the other stationery items, it is difficult to simply transpose the information from the larger formats and to continue the design style of the stationery range.

You will probably have to reduce the size of the name and/or symbol. But if you continue to use the same colours and typefaces you will still create the sense that the business card 'belongs' to the note paper, invoice and compliment slip.

STUDIO EQUIPMENT

C. J. Graphic Supplies Ltd
2-3 Gt. Pulteney Street London W1 Telephone: 01-439 3489/3517
372 Caledonian Road London N1 Telephone: 01-607 6610/6640
122/124 North End Road London W14 Telephone: 01-381 0081/0440

C. J. Graphic Supplies Ltd.
372 Caledonian Road.
Islington.
London N1
Tel: 01-607 6610/6640

With Compliments

Symbols and logos

The essence of a good symbol or logo is simplicity. This belies the fact that often they are born out of some very complicated ideas: a large amount of information is reduced into one simple visual statement.

Although they often have the same function, symbols and logos are not the same thing. A symbol is basically a picture representing an idea, while a logotype, or logo for short, is a group of letters or even a whole word which is used as a picture.

The flowing line of the Harrods logo leaves an impression of effortless sophistication, while the large 'H' reinforces the store's name. The geometric lines of the Habitat logo create a more down-to-earth feel. The store's name and character is cleverly suggested by the stylized table and chairs.

Designing a symbol
The best way to start is to make a list of visual images relating to the subject that you want to symbolize.

For instance, if your subject were related to high technology, you would start by making a list of all of the words related to that subject that you could think of: computers, electronics, micro chips, and so on, until you feel that you have

exhausted all of the possibilities. Then you take each word and try to make a simple picture from it. By the time you have done this you will probably have a fairly large amount of visual information about your subject; some obviously important. Use these elements and combine them in as many ways as you can, until you produce a good symbolic representation of your subject. Remember that the best ideas are usually the simplest.

Producing such a symbol can be a very long and tortuous process; designers often say that it is one of the hardest items to design.

There are other types of symbol, perhaps not so sophisticated, but effective none the less. A highly refined and simplified pictorial representation – for instance, those used on road signs or the celebrated Olympic Games symbols – are good examples of how a complicated idea can be reduced to a diagram which economically communicates that idea.

The Adult Literacy Association is an organisation which teaches adults to read and write. This simple arrangement of shapes clearly represents a person reading a book.

Logos
There is little difference between some symbols and logos. Company trade marks, for instance, which use the company name's initial letter transformed into a relevant image combine elements of both the symbol and the logo.

The Kelloggs cereal logo works in a straightforward way, using the company's name in a wholly factual manner and avoiding any abstract connotations.

The Dunhill cigarettes logo also works on a factual level, but the elongated letters add a faint abstract touch by suggesting a cigarette.

IBM Computers have used their initials rather than their full name on this logo. The type's technical appearance suggests the company's product.

El Al Airways also use their initials on this logo. The abstract positioning of the letter 'A' suggests an aeroplane's tail and reinforces the company's role.

McDonald's Foods have combined both factual and abstract approaches in their logo. Besides using their full name they have integrated a giant 'M' into the design.

The combination of an abstract steering wheel and a business name in this logo cleverly advertises the Volkswagen automobile company.

Olympia International's abstract logo incorporates the company's initials in a design that suggests a typewriter spool, thus advertising the firm's product.

Alitalia's logo uses an abstract approach that, like El Al, suggests the tail of an aeroplane. However, the company's initials are less obvious.

The Mercedes Automobile logo is completely abstract and resembles a car steering wheel. Elegance is implied by the design's simplicity and symmetry.

The Shell Petroleum Company relies entirely on an easily identifiable symbol in this logo. In a more esoteric way, the shell suggests oil's origin as a fossil fuel.

Bell Telephone's logo simultaneously reinforces the company's name by using the bell shape, and suggests the ringing of a telephone.

The logo for the Heating and Ventilating Contractors' Association ignores their initials, but stresses their importance in house insulation and ventilation.

Greetings cards

The first greetings cards to be made in any numbers were Valentine's Day cards during the latter part of the eighteenth century. They soon became very elaborate, with lacy embossed designs and full-colour illustrations, and complicated combinations of different materials and pictures. By the time the postal system was established in the mid-nineteenth century, the Valentine card had become extremely popular.

Within a few years, however, the popularity of the Valentine card was overtaken by that of the Christmas card. The sentimental images of horse-drawn coaches in the snow, robins, holly and mistletoe are still as popular today as they were all that time ago.

It has become a popular practice today to make your own greetings cards. It is a perfect way of displaying your talents and interests, in conjunction with a token of friendship or love.

Photomontage and collage

It is often possible to find complete or parts of images that you can simply cut out and stick on to suitable card or paper. If you enjoy making this kind of photomontage picture, plan for the future by scanning old magazines before you throw them away and cutting out any interesting pictures. Making a photomontaged card is very simple if you have a stock of 'cuttings' to leaf through when you are composing your picture.

Do not make the picture over-complicated: use only two or three elements.

Collage is distinct from photomontage in that it uses coloured or textured papers cut into shapes to make up an image. The paper, either cut or torn, can be positioned so that areas of colour and tone are built up, perhaps into a recognizable image. This technique often has a child-like quality, but do not be put off by that: many famous artists have used collage in their work.

A SELECTION OF SIMPLE GREETINGS CARDS

Making your own greetings cards gives a personal touch that will be much appreciated. The range is as wide as your imagination, but the price can be as low as you wish.

Other techniques

Photomontage or collage techniques can be used in conjunction with drawing. Or you can simply draw or paint the picture that you want. A rather devious tactic used by those who are not very confident of their own drawing is to employ a young child to do the drawing for them – any lack of drawing skill is then instantly forgiven by the recipient!

Anything that gives the card a unique quality adds to its potency: for instance, a carefully mounted pressed flower or a small piece of fine lace can transform an ordinary greetings card into a treasured possession. Or you can cut shapes into the front of the card to reveal part of the inside, or cut around the edge of a drawn shape.

Folding cards

Most cards have an illustration on the front of a folded piece of card, with a space for a pre-printed or written message on the inside.

However, there are other ways to fold the card. With a concertina fold, for instance, you can fold the card as many times you like, and can continue the same illustration across the card to produce a series of illustrations which are only revealed as the card is unfolded.

Another suitable type of fold is the gate fold: the card is folded so that the outside edges meet in the centre. When the card is opened the image on the front splits to reveal another image or a message inside.

Pop-up cards

The most spectacular and complicated cards to produce are 'pop-up' ones, where a seemingly flat picture suddenly becomes three dimensional. A pop-up card is successful if an appropriate image has been used, and if it has been executed skilfully. The simplest way of achieving this exciting effect is as follows:

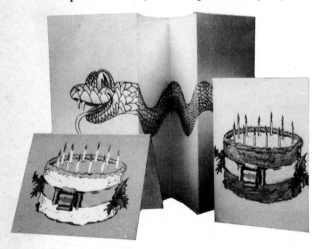

Cards can be folded simply to have an illustration on the outside and a message inside – or you could be more ambitious. Try a concertina fold where you keep on folding the card so that it unfolds gradually revealing more of the illustration.

Fold a simple rectangle of card across the middle. Then mark on it two equal lines perpendicular to the fold, which extend an equal distance on either side of the fold.

Now cut along these lines with a sharp knife. Fold the card along the crease and, as you do so, push up the cut shape gently in order to reverse the crease in that section.

This creates the most basic type of pop-up card by creating a simple support for more complicated shapes, which can be glued to it. Make sure that the whole card will fold successfully to fit into an envelope. The outside of the card can be decorated by any of the methods described, and enough space should be left inside for a message.

EXAMPLES OF LINOCUT CARDS

Linocut cards are the cheapest way of producing a fairly large number of cards (see chapter 10).

Hand printing

Producing as many as 20 or more hand-made cards is extremely time consuming. If you cannot afford to have them printed professionally you can produce them yourself using a screenprinting process (see chapter 10): an easy and enjoyable way of making a number of professional-looking cards cheaply.

Printed cards

There is a certain category of cards which need to be professionally reproduced in some way, either because of the quality required, or because hand-made cards would give the wrong impression. Formal party invitations; wedding invitations; tickets (for charity events and so on); change of address cards; all these look best if they are professionally reproduced.

Invitation cards

Invitation and other formal cards, although varying in size and in the use of typeface and colour, tend to have a basic layout and format which is rarely deviated from. This traditional, centred style (see below) is ideal for setting out short lines simply and elegantly, and it allows for changes of type size and even typeface.

The typefaces traditionally used for invitation cards are those which simulate copperplate script or which have a distinctly rounded quality.

It is possible to buy pre-printed cards of all kinds: the most common is the wedding invitation. Many small printers will show you a catalogue with a wide variety of designs from which you can choose. But most of these pre-printed cards are undistinguished and look mass-produced.

There are two alternatives: you can either commission a print shop to produce a design for you, or you can design your own card.

Whichever you choose, you will have to decide on the message to be included in the invitation. Whether or not you use the traditional wording used in formal invitations you must make it clear who it is from, who it is to, what it is for, and where and when the event is taking place. You might also want the recipients to notify you whether they are coming, or to advise them of any special circumstances (the type of clothes they should wear, for example).

Mr and Mrs J. Fawley
request the pleasure of the company of

....

at the marriage of their daughter
Cynthia to Mr Terence Crabb
at the parish church of Saint Marys, Luton
on Saturday 1 September at 12 noon
Reception at the South Lodge Hotel, Dunstable

There are many styles of formal invitation cards, although most use a similar, centred, layout. The occasion of the invitation is usually indicated outside, leaving room for the message inside.

If you are designing your own card, you will almost certainly find that the centred style of layout is the most useful for this kind of information. It also makes it easier typographically because it allows you to make a visual emphasis with line breaks. The actual wording of a wedding invitation would be:

Mr & Mrs J Fawley request the pleasure of the company of .... at the marriage of their daughter Cynthia to Mr Terence Crabb at the parish church of Saint Marys, Luton on Saturday 1 September at 12 noon. Reception at the South Lodge Hotel, Dunstable.

When the wording is centred, the appropriate line breaks will punctuate the statement and separate out all the information. In addition, to give even more emphasis to the really important parts of the message, you could set the names in a larger type size or use capital letters.

This same principle can easily be applied to almost any type of invitation or greetings card.

The typeface you choose will depend on the relative formality of the wording and on the type of event the invitation is for.

The wedding invitation (opposite) is set in a traditional typeface and reflects the formal quality of the occasion. The examples below are far less formal, using lively layouts and less conventional typography.

If they were changed around, the wedding invitation would look like a joke and the party would suddenly be transformed into a formal function. For even less formal cards you could use your own handwriting or hand lettering.

Both letterpress and offset litho are used to print cards. Thermography is a suitable way of producing formal invitations, as is blind embossing (see page 64). Artwork for the printer should be prepared in the usual way (see instructions in chapter 9).

When compared to the formal wedding invitations on page 76 these party invitations appear brightly informal and full of life. They convey a feeling of fun and enjoyment.

6. POSTERS, WALLCHARTS AND BANNERS

When designing items that will be viewed from a variety of distances, one of the most basic problems is how to ensure that the scale of lettering is correct.

The words you are reading on this page are about 50 cm (20 inches) away from your eyes. The x height of the letters is about 0.3 cm (⅛ inch).

If you increase the distance from which you are reading from 50 cm (20 inches) to 50 metres (164 feet), then you would have to increase the size of the x height of the lettering from 0.3 cm (⅛ inch) to about 12.5 cm (5 inches) to get the same ease of reading.

It is always best to do a test on any lettering you are going to use. Decide on a 'typical' distance from which it will be read and then try some different sizes to see which is the most suitable. If in any doubt, go for the larger size.

In addition, the letters not only need to be larger but they must be further apart from each other. Err on the generous side: more space, not less, between letters.

DISTANCE CHART

Distance of viewer from letters		Sensible minimum size of 'x' height	
(metres)	(feet)	(cm)	(inches)
10	33	2.5	1
20	66	5	2
30	99	7.5	3
40	131	10	4
60	197	15	6
80	262	20	8

The figures in the table are only approximations.

They will change according to the particular kind of letterform and typeface you are using. This table refers to Helvetica, which is a particularly clean and clear typeface developed specifically for easy legibility.

If you are using fine delicate lettering or a highly decorated typeface, then the sizes will have to be increased.

If the sign is either in a high or low position, the letters will be distorted for the viewer. This must be compensated for.

A banner is one of the most effective ways to make a statement. Because the messenger appears simultaneously with the message, onlookers are forced to take note and challenged to react.

Wallcharts

A wallchart is an effective way of conveying more than one piece of information to an audience. For example, it would be ideal in circumstances where you needed to explain a process with a number of stages, such as bread making to a cookery class. First, you would demonstrate the process. But not all the audience may be able to remember the different steps, or the order in which to do them. A prominently displayed wallchart depicting the process in simple terms could be used as a reference by the whole class, either individually or as a group, when repeating the process themselves.

A wallchart is also useful for presenting information to the casual observer. Charts explaining various methods of loft insulation, say, or showing birds that can be spotted in the area, might be placed in a local library. The information will be absorbed by a passing audience who are presented with information which they find useful or interesting. They should be designed to catch the attention of passers-by.

The *positioning* of a wallchart is particularly important. A wallchart showing the safety procedures for using machinery in a workshop, for instance, must be placed close to the machinery and be clearly visible at all times. It needs to be on a surface uncluttered by other notices, and to be positioned at a suitable height for viewing easily.

A wallchart is designed on a grid system similar to that of a magazine layout (see pages 93–7). But, remember, the amount of information that can be presented is restricted, because usually the people reading the chart will be standing up: if they become tired or disinterested they will very probably walk away. For the same reason, the design of the wallchart should ensure that the information is presented in such a way that it is easy to follow and also easy to understand.

A wallchart for children.
This chart showing a space shuttle can easily be made by finding appropriate drawings and photographs from newspapers and magazines. Cut these out and stick them on to a large sheet of paper. The caption material can be applied by hand lettering or stencil. Spray the completed chart with a fixative to prevent the lettering and drawn images from smudging.

This is an inexpensive way of producing a wallchart to brighten up a nursery or classroom. Children can participate in the creation of this type of chart by either producing it themselves or by choosing the pictures.

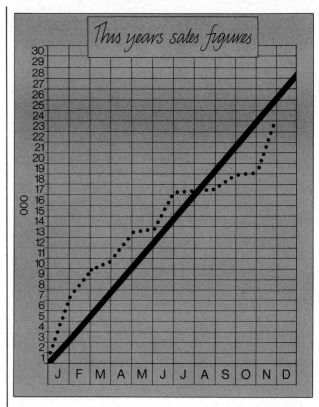

A nature chart

This nature chart has been designed to serve as both decoration and a source of information about the leaves themselves.

By applying the leaves to areas of the wallchart the difference in the shape, colour and texture of each is clearly seen. Dry the sprigs or leaves carefully and then stick them on to the paper or card with a small amount of glue – a spray adhesive would give the lightest and most even covering. When the glue has dried, shake any excess material off. Captions or labels can be handwritten or typed on to paper and then glued in the appropriate position. Dry transfer lettering or stencils can also be used.

Remember that any vegetable materials to be used such as wild flowers or leaves must be dried or pressed first. To protect the chart from dust and dirt, cover it carefully with a clear material such as self-adhesive acetate.

Office wallcharts

This example shows a graph made from materials available at good stationers and graphic supply shops, and is particularly appropriate to small businesses, where only small amounts of time and money may be available to prepare such a display. Dry transfer lettering, stencil lettering, coloured labels, pre-cut shapes such as circles and squares in a range of colours, can all be mounted on to various plain or coloured papers or graph papers to quickly create a graph or chart. It should be noted though, that the life of such a wallchart is limited, as labels fade and peel off. However, the wallchart can be covered with a clear self-adhesive film, to protect the surface.

Printing a wallchart
If you require several copies, or even just a small number of professional-looking wallcharts, you will have to prepare artwork for printing (see chapter 9). One of the best methods of printing a wallchart is screenprinting and you can do this yourself at home (see page 138).

Although one thinks of printed items as permanent, remember that printing inks fade, particularly when placed in direct sunlight. Laminating (that is, the application of a thin transparent coating to the wallchart) will prevent the ink from fading for some time. It also protects the paper on which the wallchart has been printed, and enables the chart to be wiped clean of dust and other marks.

Posters

The difference between a poster and a wallchart is not necessarily one of style, size, or density of information, but of the time span over which either is useful in terms of the information it conveys. For instance, the notice depicting ways of making bread falls into the category of wallchart, because the information it is presenting is timeless. But one notice containing the information that an exhibition will take place on a particular day can be categorized as a poster: after the exhibition is over the poster becomes redundant. It may still be a beautiful object, but its actual function has changed from informative to decorative.

In addition, the audience coming into contact with a poster does so accidentally, and, depending on the effectiveness of the design, will either notice it, or remain unaware of the information it contains.

Although every design problem is unique, and the particular requirements of one poster design will differ from another, there are a number of basic points to consider.

Design tips for a poster
Initially, the poster must communicate in an extremely direct way, in order to attract attention. The amount of information to be carried may vary from very little to a great deal, but in all cases the impact of the poster must be established at first glance.

1. *What exactly do you wish to communicate?*
You must have a crystal clear idea of what you wish to say to your audience: consider every aspect of the information you have to present and isolate the single most important factor, which will convey your message most directly.

2. *Does the image say this clearly?*
You must present this central idea either with an image or typographically. Again it is important to test each idea that occurs to you against this question. If the idea can be misinterpreted, it will be; discard it. Whether you decide to use a humorous, a dramatic or an abstract image it must convey your idea quickly and accurately.

3. *Do the words get to the point?*
Is the most important verbal information the most prominent? Is all the subsequent information presented logically and in relation to type size, weight and position? You must lead the audience from one piece of information to the next in order of importance. If, at any point, the information becomes confusing, or difficult to extract, the effectiveness of the poster will be greatly reduced.

4. *Would you look at this poster twice?*
Unfortunately it is quite possible to fulfill all of the above requirements and still produce a boring and thus ineffective design. That spark of imagination must come from you, the designer. Apart from these basic criteria, poster design really obeys no law. Successful designs are the product of imagination, coupled with the original and perceptive analysis of the information to be presented. Any trick could, and should, be used, because the important thing is for the poster to be noticed.

Do not be fooled by the apparent simplicity of the two posters on the right. Although they may look easy to achieve, their concepts and designs are highly sophisticated. Part of their effect lies in the way in which both companies have identified their contrasting markets.

The poster advertising 'L'Atlantique' works by using a stylized image of a steamship in such proportion and scale that it immediately becomes a dramatic and arresting image. Because of the strength of the image, very little accompanying text is required. The poster for the National Theatre, on the other hand, clearly shows that image is not a prerequisite for a successful poster. This dynamic arrangement of type, the simple use of colour (the original uses black type on a red background), the bold contrast of type sizes, and the arrangement of the lettering are quite enough to engage our attention.

For women. Stretch denim that keeps its shape.

Producing a single poster

When producing a single poster, the range of materials and techniques which can be used is extremely wide. The availability of materials, the amount of time you have to produce it, and the situation in which the poster will be displayed must all be considered. The following methods are all useful, and can be used by themselves, or in any combination. Remember, if you are intending to display your poster outside, unprotected from the weather, any water-based material, paint or ink, will be affected not only by rain but by moisture: a heavy dew or mist can cause pigments to run.

Design and artwork procedure
1. Rough out ideas at a small size to start with (see pages 26–8). Work on these until you are satisfied that one is the most appropriate and then draw it full size, making any necessary adjustments to the size or position of the elements. When you are satisfied with the design, make a full-size rough (see page 28) with all the

To produce a poster, first rought out a number of design ideas on a small scale, considering as many different approaches as possible (above). Having chosen the approach you consider the most successful, draw it out full size and experiment with the elements until you are satisfied with the result (right). Then draw out a full size rough with all the elements accurately placed in position.

elements at their correct size and in their correct positions.

2. If you are using white cartridge paper it is best to stretch it (see pages 116–7) before applying either paint or inks. If you are using coloured papers check with the suppliers that stretching the paper will not damage the colours.

3. Whether you are using paper or board, secure it to either a drawing board or a table. If you are using less than the whole area draw out the format of the poster, making sure that all four corners are square.

4. Next, trace the type off a type sheet (see pages 53–4). If you are using a stencil (see page 110) either draw in the outline of the stencil letter and fill it in; or paint the letters directly through the stencil. If using the second method be careful the paint or ink does not run beneath the stencil, blurring the edges of the letters.

5. If using dry transfer lettering, apply this in the normal way (see page 107).

Drawing is the most direct way to express an image, but it does assume a certain skill. Always

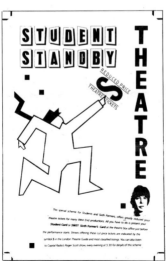

If you wish to print the poster rather than producing only one, draw out the line artwork at full size. Mark the positions of type and image and trace on headings and other copy. If you are using one or more colours, use the final full size rough as a tracing guide; place it beneath a sheet of tracing paper and block in all the areas you think most appropriate. Try a number of colour combinations until you find the most effective solution and use overlays to prepare colour artwork for the printer (see next page and chapter 9).

rough out your drawing at full size before doing the final version on the poster. Or trace an already existing image using the method described on pages 114–6. Collage can often create surprising and effective images; but care must be taken when cutting round single elements of larger photographs or illustrations.

Printing posters

For small formats and for quantities over 500, litho is comparatively cheap. It is good for reproducing small sizes of type and detailed illustrations or photographs. Screenprinting can be used up to about 594 x 841 mm, or 23 x 35 inches, and at larger sizes is relatively economic. It is best for large areas of flat colour and intensity of colour, due to the quality of ink used. Another advantage of screenprinting is that it does not require sophisticated technology and can be done at home.

Preparing two-colour separated artwork
For two-colour artwork, the various elements of the design will be contained on two surfaces: the baseboard, and one overlay (see chapter 9). Every element which prints in one colour will be mounted on to the baseboard, and everything in the other colour on to the overlay.
1. Clean the baseboard with lighter fuel to remove any grease. Secure it firmly to either a drawing board or table, and, in light blue pencil, mark in the crop marks in each corner, position the registration marks, and draw in the format area.
2. Mark any positioning guides – baselines, x-height lines, and so on – within the area to print, in light blue pencil.
3. Fix the type, and any illustrative elements which print in the same colour, to the baseboard.
4. Attach the overlay, and mark in the crop and registration marks in *exactly* the same positions as on the baseboard. Position the remaining elements (the second colour) on the overlay.

Banners

Banners can be impressive and effective when well executed. Part of the power inherent in this form of communication is that, simultaneously, they present not only the message, but also the messenger. A poster or a wallchart is displayed as a *fait accompli*. You cannot directly take issue with those responsible for what you see. Even a T-shirt or a badge can be worn discreetly, and easily covered. But a banner held high, whether it is in a moving crowd or fixed among a group of people, challenges the onlooker to take notice of the message, to give support, or to show disapproval in a particularly direct way. A banner cannot simply be ignored.

1. Draw out your design on a piece of graph paper, making any adjustments to the size or positioning of the lettering at this stage.
2. To size up the letters, take a sheet of paper the size of the banner and draw a grid of

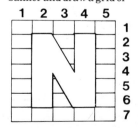

squares on it. These squares represent the squares on the graph paper; the same number of squares should be on both pieces of paper.
Over the grid of large squares draw out the shape of each letter by following the proportion of the letters drawn on the graph paper. Thus an 'N' measuring 5 squares high and 3 squares across can easily be proportionately enlarged, since it will occupy the same number and arrangement of squares on the new sheet as it did on the graph paper.

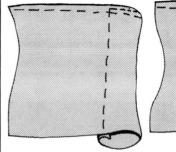

3. Cut all the sized-up shapes out of paper and arrange them on your banner. Move the letters around until the spacing and arrangement look right and then stick a strip of masking tape to the banner to give yourself a straight line along which to position the letters. Mark the position of each letter on the masking tape with a soft pencil.

4. Pin the paper letters on to the material you have chosen, and cut around the shape. If the material you are using is liable to fray, leave an extra 1 cm (½ inch) all around each letter to allow for a hem.

5. Position all the letters in their places (using the masking tape as a guide) and lightly tack them on either by sewing or stapling.

6. Finally secure the letters firmly by either sewing or stapling all the way around the edge of each one. Finally, you will have to sew or staple a narrow hem round the whole of the banner – otherwise a small tear could easily rip or fray.

ATTACHING THE BANNER TO POLES

Sewing or stapling

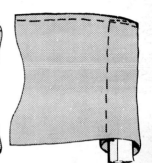

Fold each end of the banner back about 7.5 cm (3 inches) and sew or staple all the way along, and across the top edge of the fold.

This now forms a sleeve, open at the bottom and closed at the top, into which you can slip a length of wood to support your banner.

Rivets

Along the edge of the banner make equidistant holes. These must either be hemmed, or strengthened by riveting. To rivet material you will need to buy a riveter and eye rivets. Pass strong string or wire through the eyes and around the pole and tie tightly.

If your banner is very heavy it may be necessary to cut a wedge of about 5 cm (2 inches) into the pole with a saw. If the string is lodged firmly in this depression it will prevent the banner from slipping down the pole.

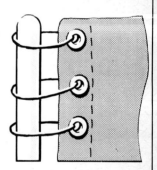

If you are considering a long march you may find it easier to carry your banner if you wind strips of towelling around the pole and fix them with carpet tacks. This will prevent the pole from becoming slippery.

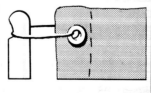

It is advisable to keep the message simple and direct. Whether you are planning to carry the banner or fix it in one spot, it may be difficult for some of your audience to get a second look. Thus the message must be clearly communicable in a short space of time. Consider, too, the circumstances under which the banner will be seen, and choose a colour scheme that will be attractive and effective out of doors. A banner with red letters on a green background announcing a country fair might look very impressive laid out on the workroom floor, but unfortunately it would not be very noticeable against a backdrop of trees or when it is in a shady position.

Ensure that any dyes you use are fast, otherwise all your hours of patient work could be ruined by a sudden burst of rain. Likewise, use durable materials to paint on which will not deteriorate quickly in poor conditions.

Banner making is quite an ambitious project, even when producing the simplest design. And it can be time consuming: if you cut corners you may well produce a banner which is unable to withstand the conditions under which it is displayed. But given appropriate attention to design and construction, a banner can be a hardy and potent symbol.

T-shirts

Screenprinting is the method generally used to produce commercial T-shirts, and if you are considering producing any quantity, this is the best method. If you are going to use a printer rather than doing it yourself (see page 133) take along a drawing of the design you are considering, and samples of the colours you wish to use. Always ask to see samples of the work produced by the printer, and check the size and quality of the T-shirts which the company uses. The production of artwork for this process is normally the same as for any design being reproduced by screenprinting (see pages 138–40), but check whether the printer requires it to be produced in any particular way.

Positioning the design

When positioning an image on a T-shirt be careful to place it in an area that the eye naturally goes to. Placed too high it can look unnatural, placed too low it can be obscured by a waist band. Trace the design out and lightly tape it to the T-shirt in the position you think best. Try the T-shirt on, and check the position in the mirror. Make any adjustments to the position and remove the T-shirt carefully, taking care not to dislodge the tracing. Make light positioning marks with dressmaker's chalk or a soft pencil on the T-shirt, and use these as guides to printing your design in the correct position.

Printing a single T-shirt

If you are producing only one T-shirt, or a very few,

The T-shirt design should occupy the centre of the garment where the eye falls naturally. If positioned too low or off-centre the design is obscured. If located too high it looks unnatural. Tape the design to the T-shirt and try the garment on before a mirror.

To make an acetate stencil, first cover the design with a sheet of thin acetate. Carefully

cut around the edges of the design with a scalpel, discarding the cut shapes.

there are a number of methods you can use based on heat sealing the dye by ironing the T-shirt after the dye has dried. However, all these methods are only

Secure the T-shirt with masking tape before positioning the stencil on top. Check that the image is located correctly and ensure that all areas of the garment not to be printed are covered. Extra masks may be needed to cover the sleeves.

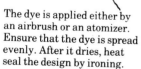

The dye is applied either by an airbrush or an atomizer. Ensure that the dye is spread evenly. After it dries, heat seal the design by ironing.

semi-permanent: despite heat sealing, the dye will fade after repeated washing. Heat-sealed items should always be ironed inside out after washing, to prevent the dye from smearing. Always follow the manufacturer's instructions when using any dyes.

Fabric crayons

These are available from most good art suppliers, and look like felt tip pens. Plan out the design first on a piece of paper. Then insert a piece of card inside the T-shirt to separate the front and back and thus prevent the dye from soaking through to the back. Mark out the design lightly on the T-shirt, and fill it in with the dye pens. When dry, iron to heat seal it.

Stencilled pigments

Using stencilled pigments is slightly more complicated. Firstly, draw up a design that is suitable for a stencil – one with too many fine lines or intricate patterns may cause problems. Cut these shapes out of a large piece of thin stencil paper or acetate. If you leave too little space between two letters or images, the dye may run beneath the stencil. Apply the dye either by airbrush or atomizer. When dry, heat seal it by ironing.

Iron-on transfers

Iron-on transfers have been commercially available for a number of years, and you can now obtain the waxed paper on which these transfers are printed. Produce a piece of artwork for your design, but in reverse (that is, as though you were looking at it in the mirror). Photocopy this image on to the transfer paper, by feeding the transfer paper through the photocopying machine instead of ordinary paper. Then iron the transfer on to the T-shirt in the normal way. Images applied to T-shirts in this way fade after only a very few washes.

Potato cuts

Dyes can, of course, be used in combination with any stamping system, such as potato cuts or a rubber lettering system.

Potato cut T-shirts

1. Cut a potato in half, and with a scalpel carefully mark out the shape you wish to print, pressing down to a depth of at least 0.5 cm (¼ inch). Remember that if you are cutting out letters, these must be reversed.

2. Cut away the surface area of the potato you do not wish to print.

3. You are now left with a cut out shape standing at least 0.5 cm (¼ inch) from the edge of the potato.

4. Stain the raised surface of the potato with dye applied with a paintbrush.

5. Press the inked surface firmly on to the T-shirt.

6. Heat seal the design by ironing.

Appliqué T-shirt design

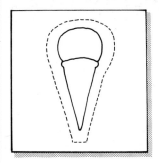

1. Draw elements of the design out on paper, and cut round these, leaving a margin around the edge.

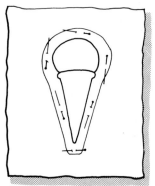

2. Pin the paper cut-outs to the material to be sewn on to the T-shirt.

3. Cut around the design, either along the edge of the design, or 1 cm (½ inch) outside it if you wish to hem each piece.

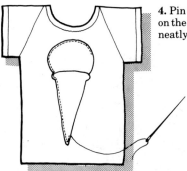

4. Pin the material in position on the T-shirt and hem it on neatly.

Stickers and Badges (Pins)

These can be used for quite practical purposes or simply for fun, but once again the constraints of space, and the random way in which an audience comes into contact with a message presented in this format, place certain restrictions on the content. The more instantly understandable the information is, the more effective.

Stickers

A sticker can be produced in a variety of sizes and colours. The material used to print on is an adhesive-backed paper, available in a range of colours, which comes in sheets mounted on backing paper. These sheets are fed through a printing press in the same manner as ordinary paper. Using this method you can specify your sticker's dimensions to be any size smaller than the actual sheet. Obviously, the greater the number of stickers which fit on to one sheet, the lower the unit cost. As a general rule, prepare the artwork for any sticker in the same way you would for other items to be printed on an offset litho press (see pages 120–7).

Alternatively, you can use pre-cropped stickers, which are of a pre-determined size and shape, and which come in a variety of colours. This is a cheaper method of production, as the printer does not have to crop the stickers: they are peeled off the backing sheet when needed. However, there are obviously greater limitations upon your design. But these blank stickers are also useful for making one-off designs at home.

Stickers and badges come in all shapes, sizes and colours. When designing your own stickers bear in mind that your design has to fit on to a sheet which will be fed through the printing press. Obviously the smaller and simpler the design, the more will fit on to one sheet, and the lower the unit cost will be.

Badges (pins)

The most commonly used badge or pin is the circular, laminated-tin type, usually available in sizes ranging from 2.5 to 4 cm (1 to 1½ inch) in diameter. These are now produced by a number of companies at relatively low prices. The initial cost always includes the price of the litho plate required for printing, but any subsequent order for the same design will be cheaper. as the plate already exists.

Prepare the artwork in the same way as for any offset lithographic work, but allow for the lip by leaving a border of at least 0.3 cm (⅛ inch) around the edge of the design.

Blank badges (pins) are available in a number of sizes and colours. These are ideal if you only want to produce a small number. Use dry transfer lettering, and then lightly spray them with fixative.

Stationers also stock a range specially designed to be used at trade fairs and conferences. These usually consist of a piece of light card inserted in a plastic cover to which a safety pin is attached. The card can be slipped out, and a message, or name and position, written on it. The card is then replaced in its cover. This is a relatively inexpensive and effective way of producing a small number of badges or pins for a specific occasion.

Badges (pins) can be bought blank if you only want a few, or professionally produced to your own design at relatively low cost.

7. DESIGNING BOOKLETS AND MAGAZINES

Like stationery and cards, booklets and magazines are usually read at no more than arm's length. This means that the size of type, line length and illustrations are governed by what can be seen comfortably at that distance. Magazines and booklets differ from stationery and cards, however, in that they are made up of a number of pages, all of the same size. Whereas a simple, single-page price list or notice, for instance, can be designed as an individual item, booklets and magazines have to be approached differently. Even though the pages inside may carry different types of information, each one cannot be designed entirely separately—they must be designed around a common system, so that when all the pages are assembled together a sense of unity exists. The unity can be quite subtle when seen in a mass market magazine which has a wide variety of column widths, type and illustration sizes, or quite obvious in a directory or catalogue. In both cases, however, the graphic designer uses a common system, or device, for constructing each page. The device is called a grid.

Grids and formats

The grid is no more than a ruler – a way of dividing up a space into a commonly understood system with a commonly understood language. It is useful to designers because it enables them to work quickly and accurately, and it provides others – printers, typesetters, illustrators – with accurate information in a way that is not open to misinterpretation.

Different types of information require different treatments on the page to ensure that the information is presented to best advantage. Both a paperback novel and a telephone directory are made up of pages of type. But there the similarity ends. They are designed quite differently because of the nature of the information contained within them. It would be very difficult to understand a novel if it was produced in the type size and short columns used in the telephone directory. And it would be equally difficult to extract the relevant information from a telephone directory in which the names, addresses and numbers were presented in continuous lines, rather than being listed.

The type of grid and the *format* (page size) are, to a certain extent, dependent on each other,

When designing the layout for your page bear in mind the type of information that it will carry, as this will affect the grid used. In the two examples above, for instance, of a telephone directory and a novel, the two contents would be impossible to read if they were transposed. Long passages of continuous prose need a fairly wide measure to let the eye run on. Long lists, on the other hand, need constant breaks if they are to be easily read.

and both must be chosen in the light of the information to be presented.

Imagine you are dealing with a continuous piece of unillustrated prose. The simplest, most direct way of presenting this information on a printed page will be the most effective. Therefore it is logical to choose a suitable length of line – one containing between 60 and 70 characters is calculated to be the optimum line length for a continuous piece of prose – and place blocks of those lines on an appropriately sized piece of paper. But if the material is illustrated, it will be treated differently. The artwork or photographs might fit within this very simple scheme, but if you have caption material (information relating directly to the illustrations), they will be of subsidiary importance to the main text. You would then have to fit two quite different categories of information into a grid system which had been designed for only one size of type, across one length of line.

To differentiate between the different categories, you could set the captions in italic type, or type of a different weight to that of the main text. Or you could employ rules to section off the captions, or evolve a system of leaving line spaces between captions and text. Alternatively a combination of these devices could be used. In some cases this might be the most efficient way of coping with the problem; in others it might be misleading and confusing.

A clearer way of differentiating between the types of information might be the use of different sizes of type, set to different measures. This obviously requires a more sophisticated grid structure; one, for example, with a length of line which can be split into two equal parts. This system enables you to choose one length of line for the caption material, and another for the main text, clearly showing two separate but complementary types of information on the page.

Dealing with four different, yet related types of information would be more complicated:

1. A few short pieces of text which need to be very strongly emphasized.

2. Longer passages of continuous text.

Although this spread is based on a straightforward grid – a single column for running text and a wide margin for caption and other material – it is flexible enough to contain all the elements – illustration, map, text, captions, and heading – in a lively layout.

3. A number of illustrations which will be reproduced in sizes varying from very small to full page.

4. Caption material for photographs.

These requirements can obviously not be met by the two-grid systems already mentioned, but need a more refined and flexible structure: one which can encompass small areas of type and illustrational material, long sections of text, large illustrations and a third category of words.

Designing a grid system

Usually grids are drawn up as a double-page spread; that is, with both left- and right-hand pages placed as they are when a book is opened.

There are a number of ways of splitting up a standard page area. A useful rule of thumb is that the more diverse the information is, the more flexible the grid needs to be. The techniques of drawing up a grid are shown on pages 95-7. But first you need to grasp the specific mathematics of particular grid systems. These basic principles are quite easy to apply, and, once mastered, you will find no problem in designing quite complex grids.

When dealing with one particular format, but a number of different lengths of line within it, remember that each length of line will require an appropriate size of type. As explained in chapter 4, a rough guide is to make the type size half the length of the measure; that is, a suitable type size for a line 16 picas long would be 8 point. Another general rule is to allow no less than 30 characters a line and no more than 70. There is no need to define the particular type sizes any more accurately than this for the moment; the chief concern is the flexibility of column widths, and the simple mathematics on which this is based.

It is usual, for reasons of accuracy of measurement, to calculate column widths in numbers of whole picas, and for there to be not less than a whole pica between any two columns. Occasionally column widths are calculated to the nearest ½ pica, and even less frequently to the nearest ¼ pica. However the same mathematical principles apply, and so the following examples are calculated to the nearest whole pica. All the examples are suitable for a page size of 210 × 297 mm or 8½ × 11 inch.

A basic grid for an A4 page
A 41-pica grid

A one-column grid
The simplest form of grid: an area on the page 41 picas wide and 60 picas deep, allowing only one length of line.

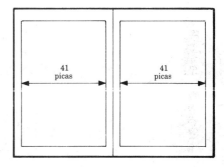

A two-column grid

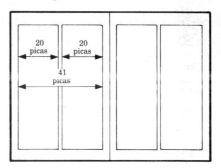

The same area on the page, but made twice as flexible, by splitting the 41-pica column into two equal columns of 20 picas each, separated by a

1-pica gutter. This allows two different lengths of line:
– 41 picas across the full measure.
– 20 picas across one column of two-column grid.

A three-column grid

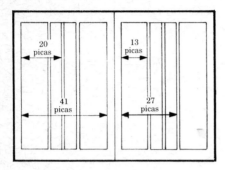

The same area as before, but again made more flexible, allowing four lengths of line:
– 41 picas across the full measure.
– 20 picas across one column of the already existing two-column grid.
– 13 picas across one column of the three-column grid.
– 27 picas across two columns of the three-column grid (that is, 13 picas multiplied by 2, plus the 1-pica gutter).

   The three-column grid could again be split into six columns of 6 picas each, with five 1-pica gutters between each column. Although a 6-pica measure is somewhat short for any amount of continuous copy, this flexibility of the columns can be extremely useful, for instance when trying to organize tabulated material (see page 69) within a common system.

   The line length nearest to 41 picas which can be similarly sub-divided would be one of 35 picas. This can be split into two equal columns of 17 picas each, with a 1-pica gutter between them; then into four columns of 8 picas with three 1-pica gutters. The same length of line can be split into three columns, each of 11 picas, with two 1-pica

gutters; that can be divided into six columns of 5 picas, with five 1-pica gutters.

A 39-pica grid
A line 39 picas long can be split into different, yet equally flexible ways.

A one-column grid
The simplest form of grid: one column of 39 picas.

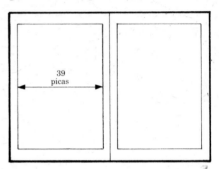

A two-column grid

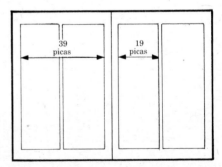

This 39-pica column can be split into two lengths, allowing lines of:
– 39 picas across the full measure.
– 19 picas across one column of the two-column grid.

   However, this length of line cannot be split into three equal line lengths comprised of whole picas. To subdivide the line length equally, 1 pica would have to be split into thirds, which is an inaccurate and therefore unsatisfactory measurement. But the two 19-pica columns can themselves be divided into two easily.

A four-column grid

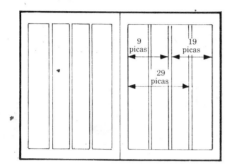

The same line length of 39 picas is split into four columns, again allowing four different lengths of line:
– 39 picas across the full measure.
– 29 picas across three of the four columns.
– 19 picas across two of the four columns.
– 9 picas across one of the four columns.

A five-column grid

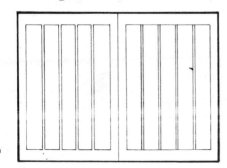

The 39-pica line can also be split into five equal parts of 7 picas each, with 1-pica gutters between each column giving five line lengths to the above four-column grid, and still remain within the same area:

– 39 picas across the full measure.
– 31 picas across four columns.
– 23 picas across three columns.
– 15 picas across two columns.
– 7 picas across one column.

From the above examples you can see that quite complex grid systems can be evolved in a quite straightforward way. When you choose a length of line that can be suitably subdivided, you allow yourself the freedom to position more than one type of information, using various combinations of line length and type size, so that each category of information is presented as effectively as possible.

Page layout

For a typical magazine article, various types of information should be identified and their relative importance assessed. Once you have done this, you can begin to make the various design decisions.

Assessing the material
The types of information to be dealt with can be split into two categories: words and pictures.

All magazine articles are comprised of at least two different types of information – the title and the text – and often there are more categories:

1. Title.

2. Introductory matter. Usually a very brief indication of what the article is about, often including credits for the writer, and possibly a photographer or illustrator.

3. Main copy.

4. Subheadings. These are headings, subsidiary to the main title, which head sections within the main text.

5. Captions.

6. Tabulated matter (any comparative information, often numerical, which is presented in the form of either tables or charts).

7. Any other information which is subsidiary to the main text, but is neither captions nor tabular matter; for example, a list of relevant addresses or publications.

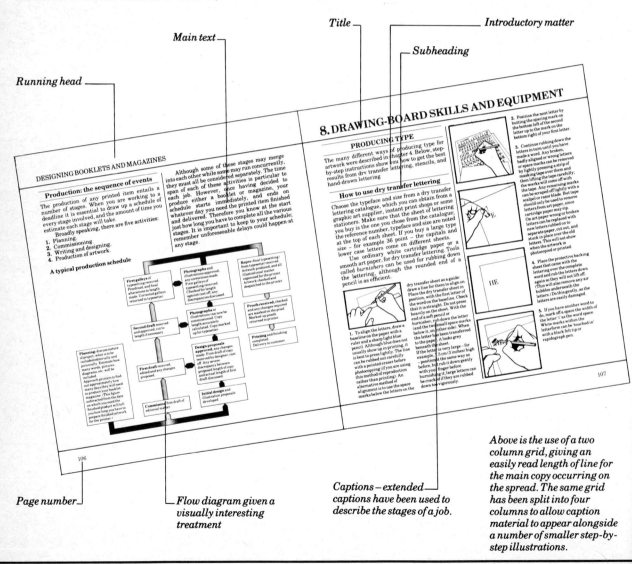

Running head

Main text

Title

Subheading

Introductory matter

Page number

Flow diagram given a visually interesting treatment

Captions – extended captions have been used to describe the stages of a job.

Above is the use of a two column grid, giving an easily read length of line for the main copy occurring on the spread. The same grid has been split into four columns to allow caption material to appear alongside a number of smaller step-by-step illustrations.

The quality of illustrative material can be divided roughly into two sections:

1. The informative, that is, an illustration or photograph used to explain specific information: a map, for example.

2. The evocative, that is, an illustration or photograph used to attract attention and to provoke an atmosphere or feeling about a subject.

These two categories often overlap, but it is useful to identify the types of illustrations, and establish their importance (their relative sizes and positions) in the design.

When considering what illustrative material to include (see chapter 4), do not assume the reader will be as well acquainted with the subject as you are. For instance, suppose you wished to design a booklet which would inform people of the evening classes to be held at a local school. You may know where the school is located. So the question of whether to include a map indicating the position of the school might go unasked, although it might be necessary.

You might decide that, while a map should be included, it is neither an attractive image, nor does it inform about the nature of the meeting. Thus you need a second image as well: one which perhaps takes precedence in size and position to the map. Thus, the images to be used can be sorted out into appropriate sizes, and their relative importance within the design judged.

Designing a magazine article

Imagine you have to design an article, with text and images, to be contained on one double-page spread. The first thing to consider is the element which is least flexible. As a general rule, this is usually the amount of copy to be included. So the first step is to cast off the copy (see pages 45-9) and then, once you have chosen a type size, find out exactly how much of the area at your disposal this occupies.

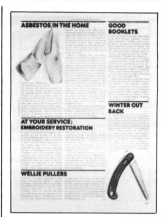

The simple use of a three column grid presents information in a direct, uncomplicated way. The grid enables the designer to use different picture sizes, while maintaining a constant column width for the type.

A four column grid allows more flexibility and a livelier lay-out, more suited to an informal subject matter.

A number of short entries of copy can be accommodated by the five column grid, which allows general information to cross three columns and picture captions to cross two.

Producing an accurate layout

1. Place a sheet on which you have drawn up your grid under the top sheet of a pad of tracing paper. With a drawing pen or a fine felt tip, trace the format of the double-page spread on to the top sheet of tracing paper, marking in the centre line along which the spread folds. Use a depth scale (see page 38) to mark out the number of lines the copy occupies. This gives you a good idea of how much of the area the copy fills, and how much space you have left to fit all the other elements.

2. On a fresh piece of paper draw out a number of rectangles, representing the full-sized format; approximately one-quarter of the actual size. Within these rectangles make visuals (see chapter 4), or very rough sketches of the positions you wish all the elements to occupy. At this stage, indicate the various pieces of the design with small shapes: a block for the headline, columns for the type and empty rectangles for the illustration areas. Repeat this procedure a number of times, trying out different arrangements of the various elements but bearing in mind that the size of the text area must remain constant, although its shape may change. When you have arrived at a rough design which works well, you can draw it out at full size.

3. On a separate sheet of paper, roughly trace

your headline from a type sheet (see page 54), and draw out the full-sized areas of any illustrations; cut all these out.

4. Take another sheet of tracing paper and again

1. Trace the format of the spread on to the top sheet of tracing paper.

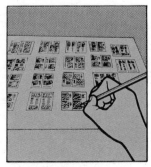

2. Draw up rectangles and make a number of visuals of your layout.

3. On a separate piece of paper trace your headline and illustrations.

4. Trace out your page format again and place the headline and illustration areas on it.

trace out the full-sized format. Allowing space for the type area, place the cut-out headline and full-sized picture areas over the grid, according to your rough design. At this stage, again try different arrangements, as the initial small sketch may need some alteration; for instance, the headline might appear too large, or the size of an illustration might not leave enough room for a caption. This does not matter – merely make the appropriate adjustments. As you rearrange the positions and sizes of the various elements, a suitable design will gradually emerge (possibly one that had not even occurred to you when you sketched out your ideas on a small scale).

5. When you have arrived at what you consider to be the optimum solution, you must produce an accurate, working layout which will enable you to specify type sizes and illustrative areas. This layout must also be sufficiently detailed to be used as a guide to producing the artwork. Begin by drawing out accurately all the short pieces of significant type – headline, introductory matter, subheads, and so on – to the size and weights (that is, the darkness of type) you wish to use. Do this on a clean sheet of tracing paper, although it is not necessary to position each piece of type as it will appear on the page.

6. Once again trace out the format of the grid on the top sheet of a tracing paper pad. Next take the sheet of tracing paper on which you have traced the headline and subheads, and place that between the grid and the tracing paper so that the headline appears in its proper position. Trace off the headline on to the top sheet. Repeat the process for any introductory matter, but not the subheads.

7. To indicate the position of the main text, use either a soft pencil or a grey felt tip pen and draw lines to show where each line of copy goes. These lines should sit on the baselines of the grid and extend across the width of a column. When you come to a subhead, trace it off the tracing paper as you did for the headline. Continue this process until all the main text has been lined in, and all the subheads drawn in position.

8. Next, indicate the positions of illustrations, tabulated material and any other material, by drawing boxes around the perimeters of the areas they occupy. Then either trace in the caption material, or line it in as you did the main text.

You now have an accurate layout on one sheet of paper, and you can proceed to mark up the manuscript for the typesetter, and specify sizes of illustrations or photographs in preparation for producing the artwork (see pages 120-7).

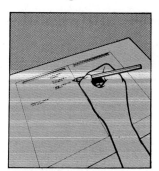

5. Trace out accurately all short pieces of significant type.

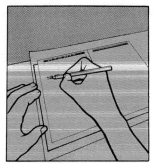

6. Trace the headline and introductory matter on to the page format.

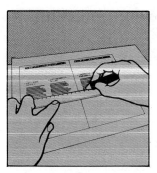

7. Draw lines to represent where each line of text goes, and trace off the sub-heads.

8. Indicate the position of illustrations by drawing boxes to the required size.

Choosing the paper size

When considering some of the factors affecting the choice of grid, the page size used was either 210 x 297 mm, or 8½ x 11 inches. However, there is no particular reason or convention why these particular sizes should be chosen.

The format of any publication should be considered in the light of various criteria: the type of information to be presented; the circumstances in which the publication will be read and the most logical size in terms of economics, production and distribution.

1. *What type of information is to be presented?*
Different information can be presented most effectively on particular grids, many of which can be accommodated within the same page area. But there are obviously certain extremes which exclude certain grids. For instance, perhaps the information to be presented requires a highly flexible structure, such as a five-column grid. If, for some reason, the page size could not be larger than 120 x 200 mm (5 x 8 inches), this would mean that you would have a column width of 4 picas for each of the five columns, which is clearly an impractical measure for anything other than tabulated material. You must either restructure the information, or enlarge the format. In most cases changing the format is probably the easier solution. But also remember factors 2 and 3.

2. *Under what circumstances will the publication be read?*
This requires close consideration: the suitability of certain formats as opposed to others will not always be clear cut. For instance, if your prospective audience has to carry around and regularly consult the publication, as in the case of a guide book to a museum, something the size of a newspaper would be unwieldy. In this case, a booklet which could be slipped into a pocket or bag would obviously be the most suitable. On the other hand, if the publication is intended to be read at leisure such rigorous constraints need not apply, and you can consider a wider range of formats.

3. *Is the most logical size practical in terms of economics, production and distribution?*
Some formats are more expensive than others. The price is partly dependent on the number of double-page spreads the printer can fit on one of the large sheets of paper that is fed through the printing press. For example, a number of double-page spreads with a page format of 240 x 350 mm (10 x 14 inches) may not fit on the printer's sheet of paper particularly well; 15 per cent of this sheet may have to be discarded. A slightly smaller format might fit a greater number of spreads on the printer's sheet with only 7 per cent wastage.

Other aspects of production should also be taken into account. It would be unwise to choose a format which could not be finished – that is, collated and bound – by your printer. The way in which the publication is to be distributed should also be considered: if you plan to send it by mail, for instance, ensure that if fits within a readily

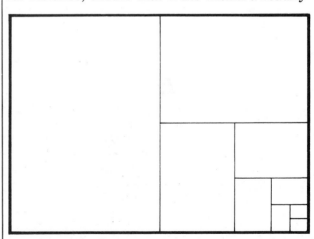

Make sure that the paper size you have chosen is not only suitable for the information to be carried, but also the most economical. Metric paper sizing works on the system of the next size being half of the one before.

available envelope.

Take all these factors into acount at the planning stage in order to avoid any alterations which, at a later stage, could be time consuming and costly.

Cover design

The cover is the first part of your magazine or booklet that the potential reader will see and, as such, is fulfilling a similar rôle to that of a poster. The function of the cover is to attract attention. Therefore the information it contains must be considered in a very different way from the information included inside the publication. The cover must be sufficiently engaging to interest people and to prompt them to pick it up and look through it. However, the two parts of the magazine or booklet are closely related, and should complement each other.

The way information from the inside of the publication and the outside is received differs considerably. You might spend five or ten minutes, or even longer, looking at a double-page spread while reading an article. On the other hand, you might look at a cover for as little as three seconds, and probably not much longer than ten seconds. The attention of the prospective reader must be engaged in that short time for there to be any chance that he or she will pick up the publication. So, within an extremely short period of time, the cover has to both attract and retain attention, and somehow suggest the contents of the magazine.

The specific theme of the publication – which is related to the reasons for producing it in the first place, and to its editorial content – must be stated strongly on the cover. For example, a magazine which is about tennis and which has a long main article on John McEnroe's approach to the game could feature an action photograph of McEnroe on the cover. But then you must make it obvious why he is singled out and why your article is more interesting than one in another magazine: you need a striking visual presentation evolved from the visual material and some short, informative, but catchy, copy about the article, and also about other items which are included.

It is often useful at this stage to list every aspect of the publication you can think of – the contents, the potential readership, personalities, and so on – and consider how each one might be utilized, both visually and verbally. From this list you will probably find that there are a number of promising ideas; it is worthwhile spending some time on each to discover which will make the most tantalizing cover stories.

Visualizing a cover

The clearest way to find out if an approach is working is to start drawing the idea out, very roughly. As in developing the layouts for the inside of the magazine, start visualizing on a small scale, say at one-quarter of the actual size. Indicate where any type matter would be placed in relation to photographs or illustrations you wish to include. Or you may decide to use only type on your cover, in which case the same procedure still applies. Always try to avoid any dogmatic preconceptions of how your design should look: it is often difficult to be objective about a design, and hard to discard an idea which initially seemed attractive but is not successful.

For you to be able to judge how effective the cover design is, it must be visualized to a high standard. Work at full size, but in pencil only, from the one or two original small-scale roughs which you feel are most promising. Roughly trace in any type and illustrations or photographs to be included, until you are satisfied that one solution is more effective than any other. Towards the end of this stage you should be tracing in and positioning any type accurately, and indicating any visual material to a similar standard (see page 28). The accurate tracing in black and white can now be used as a guide to producing the final colour visual (if you are using colour).

To make a colour visual take your final black and white layout and trace over this a number of times on separate sheets of paper. Then try out a number of colours and combinations of colours. This is a valuable exercise, as you may be surprised to find that the least promising colour combination turns out to be the most successful.

Having produced a full-sized, full-colour visual, it is often useful to try it out in the surroundings in which it will be presented to the public. For instance, if your publication is to be presented on a news-stand alongside other magazines, collect some of these together and place your mock cover among them. The type size you have chosen might be too small, or the colours you have used may not be strong enough. Once you have made any necessary adjustments, try out the amended design in similar circumstances. However time consuming and laborious, this is extremely important: a magazine with a disappointing cover will sell far fewer copies than one with an appealing cover.

To see if your design will work, roughly draw the design out and pencil in the main areas of type and illustration.

To see how effective it really is you will eventually have to produce a rough to a much higher standard.

Your cover is so important that it is worth the time and trouble to see if it will sell alongside other magazines. Collect some magazines together and lay them out as on a news stand; place yours among them. Does it stand out?

STAGES IN DESIGNING A COVER

The illustrations on the left show three stages in producing a book jacket. Once the basic design has been chosen from a number of roughs, the line work – rules and type – are accurately drawn on to the base artwork. This line work can be converted quite cheaply to a film positive, which allows you to put different colours and/or images behind it to see what the results will be.

The next stage is to choose the background jacket colour and the artwork or photographs. At this stage the illustrations can be cut out from books or magazines or roughly drawn in by hand. This stage is often used to make presentations of the cover to clients. In our example the heading is in colour, but this is an expensive embellishment at this stage.

The final illustration is a photograph of the completed jacket. As you can see, the colour has been refined and the photographs have been changed – either chosen from an agency or specially commissioned. But the design and concept has scarcely altered from the initial stage.

Production: the sequence of events

The production of any printed item entails a number of stages. When you are working to a deadline it is essential to draw up a schedule of every stage involved, and the amount of time you estimate each stage will take.

Broadly speaking, there are five activities:
1. Planning.
2. Commissioning.
3. Writing and designing.
4. Production of artwork.
5. Printing and finishing.

Although some of these stages may merge into each other while some may run concurrently, they must all be considered separately. The time span of each of these activities is particular to each job. However, once having decided to produce either a booklet or magazine, your schedule starts immediately, and ends on whatever day you need the printed item finished and delivered. Therefore you know at the start just how long you have to complete all the various stages. It is important to keep to your schedule; remember unforeseeable delays could happen at any stage.

A typical production schedule

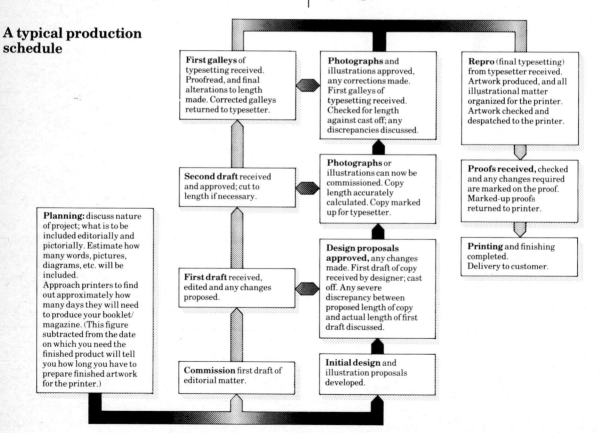

First galleys of typesetting received. Proofread, and final alterations to length made. Corrected galleys returned to typesetter.

Photographs and illustrations approved, any corrections made. First galleys of typesetting received. Checked for length against cast off; any discrepancies discussed.

Repro (final typesetting) from typesetter received. Artwork produced, and all illustrational matter organized for the printer. Artwork checked and despatched to the printer.

Second draft received and approved; cut to length if necessary.

Photographs or illustrations can now be commissioned. Copy length accurately calculated. Copy marked up for typesetter.

Proofs received, checked and any changes required are marked on the proof. Marked-up proofs returned to printer.

Planning: discuss nature of project; what is to be included editorially and pictorially. Estimate how many words, pictures, diagrams, etc. will be included. Approach printers to find out approximately how many days they will need to produce your booklet/ magazine. (This figure subtracted from the date on which you need the finished product will tell you how long you have to prepare finished artwork for the printer.)

First draft received, edited and any changes proposed.

Design proposals approved, any changes made. First draft of copy received by designer; cast off. Any severe discrepancy between proposed length of copy and actual length of first draft discussed.

Printing and finishing completed. Delivery to customer.

Commission first draft of editorial matter.

Initial design and illustration proposals developed.

PRODUCING TYPE

The many different ways of producing type for artwork were described in chapter 4. Below, step-by-step instructions show you how to get the best results from dry transfer lettering, stencils, and hand-drawn lettering.

How to use dry transfer lettering

Choose the typeface and size from a dry transfer lettering catalogue, which you can obtain from a graphic art supplier, instant print shops or some stationers. Make sure that the sheet of lettering you buy is the one you chose from the catalogue; the reference number, typeface and size are noted at the top of each sheet. If you buy a large type size – for example 36 point – the capitals and lower case letters come on different sheets.

Use ordinary white cartridge paper or a smooth art paper, for dry transfer lettering. Tools called *burnishers* can be used for rubbing down the lettering, although the rounded end of a pencil is as efficient.

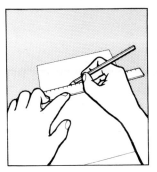

To align the letters, draw a baseline on the paper with a ruler and a sharp light blue pencil. Although blue does not usually show up in printing, it is best to press lightly. The line can be rubbed out carefully with a pointed eraser before

photocopying (if you are using this method of reproduction rather than printing). An alternative method of alignment is to use the space marks below the letters on the dry transfer sheet as a guide: draw a line for them to align on. Place the dry transfer sheet in position, with the first letter of the word on the baseline. Check that it is straight. Do not press heavily on the sheet. With the end of a soft pencil or burnisher, rub down the letter (and the two small space marks below it, on either side). When the letter has been transferred to the paper, it looks grey beneath the sheet.

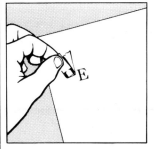

If the letter is very large – for example, 7.5 cm (3 inches) high – position it the same way as before, but rub it down gently with your finger before burnishing it; large letters can be cracked if they are rubbed down too vigorously.

Position the next letter by butting the spacing mark on the bottom left of the second letter up to the mark on the bottom right of your first letter.

Continue rubbing down the letters in turn until you have made a word. Any broken, badly aligned or wrong letters or space marks can be removed by lightly pressing a strip of masking tape over them and then lifting the tape carefully; the marks will come off with the tape. Any remaining marks can be scraped off lightly with a scalpel or razor blade. But tape should only be used to remove letters from art paper, since cartridge paper may rip.

Wrong or broken letters can also be replaced with new letters rubbed on to separate paper, cut out, and stuck in place over the old letters. This will not show when the artwork is photocopied or printed.

Place the protective backing sheet that came with the lettering over the complete word and rub the letters down again so they will not lift off. (This will also remove any air bubbles underneath the letters.) Do this gently, as the letters are easily damaged.

If you have another word to do, mark off a space the width of the letter 'i' as the word space. White marks within the letterform can be 'touched in' with a black felt tip or rapidograph pen.

A designer's basic kit

1. Selection of coloured fibre-tipped pens.

2. Markers with broad tips and large ink reservoirs; ideal for laying down blocks of colour on roughs.

3. One broad brush for applying colour washes to large areas and one fine one for more detailed work.

4. Process white.

5. Ruler with metric and imperial markings.

6. T-square.

7. Technical pens, ink and compass attachment.

8. Good quality compass that will take the attachment for a technical pen.

9. Pencils. Minimum requirement is one soft and one hard graphite pencil, and a blue pencil for drawing a grid.

10. Set square.

11. Ellipse guide.

12. French curves.

13. Lighter fuel. Ideal as a cleaning agent if you use rubber-based adhesives.

14. Spreader for rubber based adhesives. Use this device to lay a fine coat of adhesive on both surfaces to be glued.

15. Rubber based adhesive; available in cans or tubes.

16. Stick wax adhesive.

17. Masking tape.

18. Household scissors.

19. Surgeon's scalpel and a craft knife.

20. Type scale.

Not shown here, but the most important item, is the drawing board. Ensure that you get the best you can afford, with a smooth edge for the T-square. Make sure you buy the size that will handle the work you do.

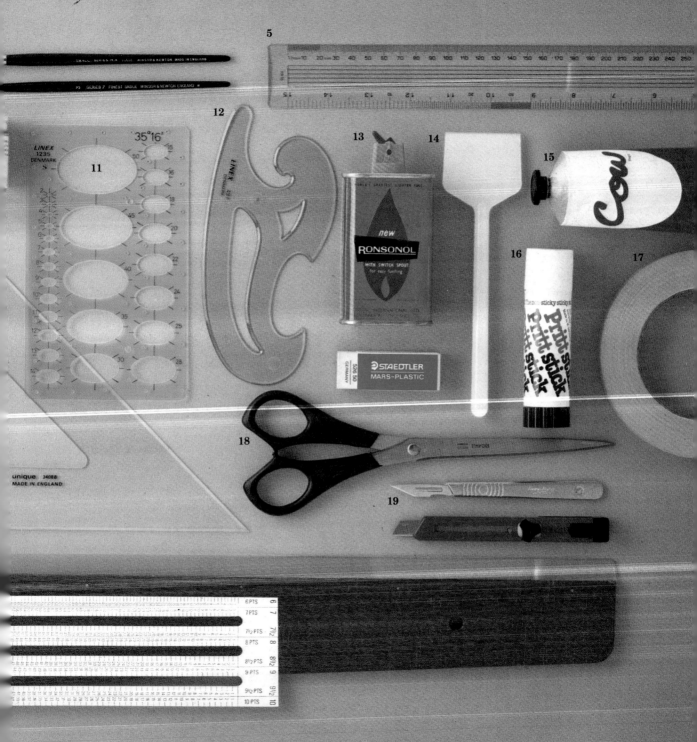

Stencilling letters

Practise with the stencil before you do the final heading to get an idea of how it works. Each stencilled letter must be drawn in stages.

If a fine felt tip pen fits through the stencil, draw the letters with this. Or use a technical drawing pen, such as a rapidograph pen, for a thinner line.

MAKING A STENCIL

Trace these letters on to stiff card and then cut along the outline. Alternatively, trace and cut out just the letters you need to make one word, and then either spray or brush paint through the stencil. If painting, use a large brush that will cover the words in one stroke.

ABCDEF
GHIJKL
MNOPQ
RSTUV?
WXYZ&

How to use a stencil

Rule a baseline lightly with a sharp light blue pencil on art paper.

Then draw a line the x height of the stencil letters above and parallel to the baseline. (Often the x height and baseline are marked on the side of the stencil.) Place the stencil over the paper in position and mark off another line where the bottom of the stencil touches the paper. Use these three lines to align your letters. Keeping your pen upright, follow the lines of your chosen letter. If you are using a technical drawing pen clean it – that is, wipe the end – before every stroke, to avoid the ink blotching. Spacing stencilled letters is difficult, because each

letter needs to have a different amount of space left either side of it. The best way to achieve even-looking spacing is by trial and error, stencilling the letters in pencil first and only going over them in ink when you are satisfied. It is a help to have a piece of similar type near you to refer to as you do it. Generally the tendency is to leave too much space between the letters; close spacing nearly always looks better than wide.

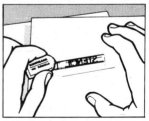

When drawing another word, leave a space the width of a letter 'n' before starting on the next word. Having completed the heading, rub out the three alignment lines and any other lines and marks.

Hand-drawn lettering

Practise these two 'calligraphic' hands with an italic pen or a broad technical pen (see page 112). Practising regularly, using the following guidelines, is the only way to learn a calligraphic hand.

Draw a baseline, x height and cap height to keep the letters the same size. Holding the pen at a consistent angle, follow the strokes in the direction of the arrows and in the order given. If you execute each stroke at the same speed, you create a rhythm: this up-and-down flow keeps the letter and word spacing even.

If some letters are badly executed, you can cut out the letters you have done well and make words by sticking them together; these can be used as artwork.

If you make a mistake on part of a letter, simply cut it out and replace it with a better one.

These are examples of the difference you can make to the appearance of the letters simply by the way you hold the pen. By changing the angle you can dramatically alter the style of lettering – 'at a stroke'.

Italic hand

To write with an italic hand, first draw lines representing the baseline, x height and cap height of the letters. Holding the pen at the same angle throughout, make the strokes in the direction and order shown. Try to establish a rhythm as you work.

a b c d e f g h i j k l m

n o p q r s t u v w x y z

Koch's capitals

ABCDEFGHIJKLMN
OPQRSTUVWXYZ

DRAWING AND ILLUSTRATION

Techniques for drawing and illustration can be divided into two basic categories: line and brush work. There is now so much equipment to choose from in both areas that it is often difficult to know what will be most useful. The descriptions and techniques given below should help you to decide which items you really need and how to use them properly.

Drawing with line

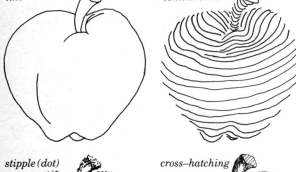

line

contour lines

stipple (dot)

cross–hatching

These four pictures are drawn in black on white: no greys were used. The greyish effect is obtained by drawing dots and lines close together.

For line drawing it is essential to have a good, smooth drawing surface such as coated art paper. The lines can be made with a variety of drawing instruments.

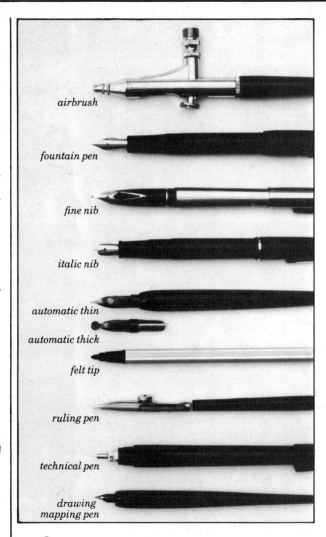

airbrush

fountain pen

fine nib

italic nib

automatic thin

automatic thick

felt tip

ruling pen

technical pen

*drawing
mapping pen*

All the above instruments are available in different sizes and can be bought from graphic suppliers or art shops. The instrument used affects the texture and thickness of the line. The strength of the lines can be varied by using watery or opaque inks on textured papers of different types.

Technical drawing pens give a consistent thickness of line and come in different widths.

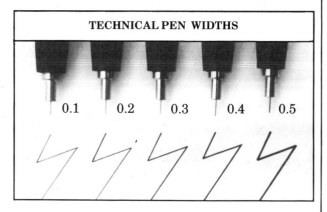

These pens are expensive and take a special type of ink: you must use the ink recommended by the manufacturer.

Felt tip pens are a bit unwieldy for drawing straight black lines accurately. They give a rounded end to the line and the black is not solid, and looks patchy when printed. Fibre tip pens are more suitable: they are harder and give a cleaner line.

Two other useful pens for drawing with line are ruling pens and drawing or mapping pens. The advantage of a ruling pen is that the width of the line can be adjusted, and therefore you can make a variety of different sized lines with the one pen. A drawing or mapping pen is very cheap and, if you keep an even pressure on it, gives a line of consistent width.

Making a straight line

To draw a clean, straight line, practise before drawing on your board. Wipe off any excess ink before you start the line and lift the pen slightly at the end of the line to avoid any ink bubbles. It is very easy to smudge the line when taking away the ruler, because the ruler is sitting in the ink. Use a ruler with an edge that does not touch the paper. Alternatively, pieces of masking tape stuck to the bottom of the ruler will lift the edge slightly and avoid smudging.

You can buy dry transfer lines on sheets in different thicknesses. They can be rubbed down in the same way as the dry transfer lettering (see page 107). Or reels of black dry transfer tape of differing thicknesses can be used. These techniques are more expensive than hand drawing, although most sheets of dry transfer lettering have lines across the top and bottom – these might be suitable for your purposes.

Dry transfer lines and corners
Letraset and other dry transfer brands make sheets of various types of corners, which are hard to draw. Alternatively, you can cut the dry transfer lines to form corners.

Drawing circles and curves

Curves can be drawn freehand, but this requires practice. It is better to use one of the following instruments.

Compasses

The main feature to look out for on a compass is a locking device which stops it moving apart when it is being used. Another useful attachment is one which holds a technical drawing pen.

Hold the rounded top of the compass when turning it: if you hold the compass too far down you might not be able to twist your hand the required distance. Compasses are used to describe circles and parts of a circle (arcs). Two straight lines can be joined with part of a circle, as shown in the diagram below, to make a curve. Find out where to put the compass point by extending the two lines: use a light pencil and draw a square. (The circle will fit into the square.)

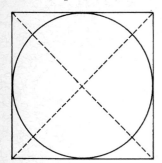

Measuring off a square is a useful technique for describing circles and parts of a circle (arcs).

Find the circle's centre by drawing two diagonal lines, from corner to corner, in light pencil. Lock the compass at the correct radius and place the compass point in the centre, where the diagonals meet.

Place the point of the attached pen on the end of one of the original lines and draw an arc round to meet the other line.

Lift the pen slightly at the beginning and the end of the curve, to avoid ink bubbles. When the ink is dry, gently rub out the pencil lines.

Use the same method – called 'measuring off a square' – to draw a complete circle. If you work on art board or paper you can correct mistakes easily by scraping them with a scalpel. 'Process white' paint, or typewriter corrector fluid can also be used to cover up mistakes: this should be applied with a fine brush.

Other equipment for drawing curves
There are other methods of drawing curves which require the use of ellipse stencils, French curves and flexicurves.

Ellipse stencils show circles in perspective. Use them when illustrating looking down on something round – for example, a wine glass. They come in a variety of sizes and shapes, so you

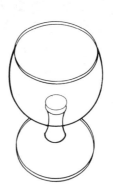 

Ellipse stencils show circles from different angles. A good exercise would be to practise

drawing wine glasses from different points of view, as shown above.

could draw your wine glass from different viewpoints as shown.

A *French curve* contains many different types of curve. It is the best instrument to use when drawing a curved corner and is also useful for drawing curved lines on a graph.

A *flexicurve* is a flexible drawing instrument: you can literally bend it to the shape you require. It is useful when drawing graphs and also means that you can control the curve.

Producing a line illustration

Although drawing an object from life, that is, with the object in front of you, usually produces the best results, it takes practice. Tracing is a more mechanical method which requires little skill to produce an attractive drawing.

Tracing from a photograph
Follow the instructions on the next page to make a professional-looking tracing. When you have finished tracing over the lines, remove the tracing paper, but do not discard it. Once you have removed it, you will probably find it impossible to reposition correctly. The tracing can be used again on another piece of board, but do

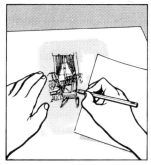

1. Secure the photograph to your drawing board and cover with tracing paper. Take a hard, sharpened pencil and lean the hand you hold it in on a separate piece of paper when drawing.

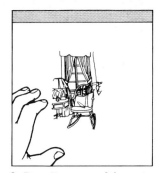

2. Draw lines around the parts of the photograph you want to trace, including shadows and other edges (for example, where colours meet); these help to define the picture. Then go over all the lines again.

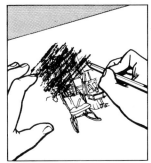

3. Carefully take the tracing off the board and remove the photograph. Place the tracing upside down over a new piece of paper. Using a soft blunt thick pencil rub the underside with steady strokes.

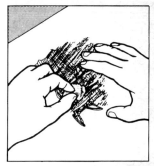

4. Rub the graphite around with a piece of cotton so there are not many pencil lines and the surface looks an even grey. (Wash your hands; the board will pick up dirty finger prints.)

5. Take a piece of board, such as Bristol board. Trim the board to size, leaving a margin of 1 cm (½ inch). Attach the tracing, graphite-side down, to the board.

6. With a hard sharp pencil and working from top to bottom, accurately go over all the lines you traced, constantly checking the original, and keeping to the lines exactly.

7. Before taking the tracing paper off the board, check to see whether you have missed any lines: shine a light on to the board at an angle.

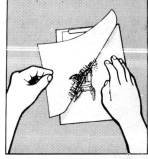

8. Remove the tracing paper cautiously, lifting one corner at a time to check again for omitted lines.

not use it more than twice as the lines become rounded, thick and unrealistic.

If you do not intend to start drawing immediately, or want to leave the drawing board at any time, cover it with a protective sheet of paper. (Keep all drinks and foodstuffs well away from the work; the same applies to small children and animals!)

How to use the tracing
You can apply numerous drawing methods to your tracing. The drawing used in the example, for instance, could have the edges of the window drawn with a ruler and pen. But this would be too mechanical and not very appropriate. It is best to use ruler-drawn lines with mechanical objects such as modern buildings and objects. Straight

lines look out of place with natural things such as trees, animals and people because they do not reflect the nature of the objects.

Line
Simply go over the traced lines with a pen, leaving out some of the detail if you wish. The lines in the foreground have been made thicker than the background lines, in order to give an impression of depth. Once the drawing is done and the ink is dry, rub out the pencil lines with a soft putty eraser.

Cross-hatching
The parts of the picture in shadow have been cross-hatched: the darker the shadow, the heavier the cross-hatching. Create grey by varying the line spacing.

Lines and textures
In this picture the lines have been drawn freehand. The textures are made by repeating a mark, such as a point or a dash. The denser textures are used in the shadows.

Hatching
A series of lines which gives the illusion of tones (greys). The lines can be in one or more direction, and they can be curved. Most effective when the lines are drawn freehand.

Dry transfers
The same principle of using textures to represent tones of grey, but using dry transfer textures and tones, which give a mechanical look because the textures are of an even consistency.

Using brushes

Brushes are the best and quickest tools for filling in large areas with paint or ink. There are an enormous variety of brush strokes which are dependent on several factors:
- The sort of paper being used.
- The sort of paint being used.
- How diluted the paint is.
- The sort of brush being used (some brushes hold more paint and so give a different stroke).
- The manner in which the brush is used (the speed and weight of the stroke).

Try the strokes out with different brushes, papers and dilutions of paint.

The three sable brushes on the right form a good collection for detailed painting. Next to that the loose hair brush applies a quick and even colour wash, while the square-end brush brings paint or ink neatly up to a straight edge. The fan brush blends adjacent colours together and the japanese brush on the left is used for adding flecks of colour.

How to stretch paper
Ordinary unstretched paper will wrinkle up when a lot of paint is applied to it, distorting the surface. Board will remain stiff, but is too expensive to use in any quantity. The solution is to stretch paper.

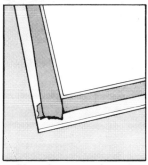

1. Place the paper to be stretched on a drawing board or table larger than the size of the paper. Cut a strip of gummed paper for each side, but longer.

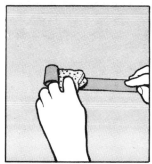

2. Wet the gummed paper thoroughly, wipe off any excess water with tissue paper or a sponge, then lay them, sticky side up, to one side.

3. Dampen the paper thoroughly with a second (clean) wet sponge, stroking it evenly over the paper.

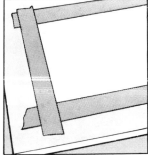

4. Place the paper on the table, smooth it, and stick it to the table with the strips of gummed paper (do not remove until the painting is completed).

Putting down flat colour

There are several ways of making a solid block of colour, over which you can draw, paint or stick things down. The simplest is to cut out coloured paper. But this is not practical when the solid colour is to be a background on a painting. Instead, use either watercolour or gouache (poster paint) on stretched paper.

Laying a watercolour wash

Use stretched paper or watercolour board and tilt it towards you. Do this by propping up one end.

Make a large quantity of the colour you want and mix it thoroughly. Once you have run out of a colour it is almost impossible to mix an identical one. About 175 to 200 g (6 to 7 oz) of colour wash should be enough if the paper size is 420 × 594mm, or 17½ × 22½ inches.

You must work fairly quickly. Dip a large thick brush into the paint, and wipe off the drips before taking it to the paper. With an even stroke, paint a line across the top of the paper.

Fill the brush up again immediately and make a second stroke, slightly overlapping the first, in the opposite direction (because the end of each stroke will have more paint).

Repeat the strokes, alternating backward and forwards. If the paint starts to drip down the page there is too much on the brush: make another stroke without refilling it. The slope of the board makes the paint sink to the bottom of the paper and the brush lines should not show. At the bottom of the page wipe off any excess.

Leave the paper to dry thoroughly before applying more paint.

Flat colour with gouache

Apply the colour to the stretched paper or board in steady vertical strokes. Then brush across. If you still have brush lines, then stroke the brush diagonally. This should leave you with a flat, even colour when dry.

Cutting techniques

There are special techniques to use when cutting artboard, typesetting proofs and so on.

For heavy materials such as artboard, scissors are not suitable and the best implement is a heavy craft knife, with which you can apply the force necessary to cut through the board cleanly and easily. Its blades, although sharp, are strong and will not break easily.

When cutting does not need to be very accurate, a pair of scissors is ideal. But they are not the best tool to use when doing detailed and accurate cutting. Instead, use a scalpel. This is a very sharp, surgical tool which must be used with extreme care, and is available at artists materials shops.

A scalpel is most useful when:
1. Cutting out very small pieces of paper for pasting up, such as when replacing one word (or even one letter) on finished artwork.
2. Cutting in intricate detail around a complex outline.
3. Cutting materials such as tints and colour films.

Tint laying

Most drawings use solid areas of black and grey as well as line. To achieve an even effect, adhesive plastic sheets of film tints are available, which can be stripped in to the drawing. As well as tints of grey a vast range of colours can be bought.

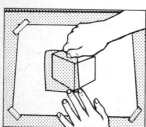

Cutting a film tint
Always lay the tint down *loosely* over the area you want to fill, otherwise the whole film will begin to stick and it can be difficult to remove. Carefully cut out the area of tint you require using a sharp scalpel or cutting knife.

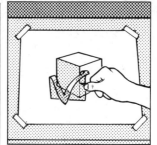

Securing the film
Remove the unwanted part of the sheet, then check that the tint is cut accurately. (If not, start again; it is difficult to add small pieces and keep the tone consistent.) Lay a sheet of paper over the artwork and burnish with a hard, smooth object over the area of tint to secure it.

It is possible to instruct the printer to lay tints on specified areas. But it is slightly cheaper to do it yourself, and the advantage of this is that you can see exactly how the drawing/diagram is going to look when printed. To do this properly requires some care; one of the most common pitfalls is allowing dust, grit and other rubbish to stick to the back of the sheet. Remember that any dirt stuck to the tint will appear on the final image, so always work in a clean environment.

Enlarging and reducing illustrations

Scaling, or *sizing,* is the term given to enlarging or reducing the size of a piece of artwork, usually a picture, for reproduction. There are two ways of scaling pictures: by calculation, and by drawing.

Scaling a picture by calculation involves measuring its length and width and multiplying or dividing these by the same number. For example, if you have a picture that is 120×70 mm (5 x 3 inches) and you want it to appear half that size on the printed job you simply divide both measurements by two. So 120×70 mm (5 x 3 inches) becomes 60×35 mm ($2\frac{1}{2}$ x $1\frac{1}{2}$ inches). If you want it twice the size, multiply both measurements by 2.

Unfortunately, the calculations are rarely as simple as a multiple of 2 or 3. For example, if there is a space for a photograph measuring 10 cm (4 inches) wide and 7.5 cm (3 inches) long, but the original photograph is 8 cm ($3\frac{1}{4}$ inches) wide and 5 cm (2 inches) long, it will be difficult to make

 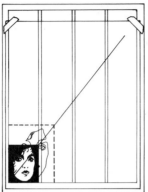

To enlarge a picture, draw a diagonal line on the overlay, joining up two corners and extending beyond the top corner. At any point along this diagonal you can draw a line at right angles to the bottom line to give you a new picture size. For example, if the picture is to be enlarged to the same width as a column on the page, extend the bottom line

on the tracing out to the full column width. From this point, draw a vertical line at right angles to the bottom line up to the diagonal. Then draw a horizontal line parallel to the bottom line from the point where the vertical line crosses the diagonal. Measure the larger rectangle to find the new reproduction size of the picture.

Use the same process to reduce your pictures; the diagonal line will not extend beyond the edge of the photograph, and the rectangle representing the new image size will be smaller than the original.

When scaling, do not mark the actual picture. Cover it with an overlay of tracing paper slightly larger than the picture, and mark that. As a positioning guide to the printer, trace a little of the picture on to the tracing paper.

enlarge to 135 mm

both dimensions fit by calculations.

In a case like this, it is usually easier to scale pictures by drawing. First trace the dimensions of the original picture on to a transparent overlay as shown above.

Colour transparencies are too small to be scaled on an overlay. Instead, use a slide projector to project the picture on to a piece of paper. By adjusting the projector, you can alter the picture until it is a good size from which to make a rough tracing. Then scale the tracing using the diagonal line scaling system, and send the printer your tracing with the size marked on it, together with the original slide.

Cropping to fit

Photographs are rarely the same size or in the same proportion as the space into which they must fit. To make an image fit, it might be possible to crop part of it without significantly affecting it.

If the photograph is to be used cropped, but without enlargement or reduction, trace the shape into which it must fit onto a piece of tracing paper and place this over it. You can move the tracing paper over the photograph until you are satisfied that you have located a part of it that will retain its meaning for the viewer. Tape the tracing paper in position, then cross out the area outside the part to be retained so that the printer knows what parts to remove. If the cropped image is to be reduced or enlarged, mark the desired final size across it on an overlay.

Crop and reduce
62mm

9. PRODUCING THE ARTWORK

In order to obtain a printed item, you almost always have to produce artwork (sometimes called the *mechanical*). The only time when it is not necessary to produce artwork is when the item is made up of type only and is to be printed by the letterpress process entirely from the printer's own standard type. If illustrations are required, or if printing is by any other method apart from letterpress – offset litho, for instance – artwork is needed. The artwork is the original from which all copies are made. The printer produces a film negative of it, and uses that to make the printing plate, block or screen.

Whereas in the letterpress process, artwork is usually only needed for illustrations or other images not available from metal type, other printing processes require artwork for the complete item – type included. All the elements have to be positioned together on a flat, stable surface, according to your design. It is best to prepare the various elements separately and then combine them, rather than working directly on to the base artwork; this allows you to position all the pieces very accurately, and gives you greater flexibility in the case of an error on one particular element.

Preparing camera-ready artwork

The elements that go to make up the printed image must be assembled on to a clean, stable surface to form the *camera-ready artwork*. The best surface is artboard, although thick, smooth white paper can be used. Artboard is specially made to take the adhesives used to glue down paper, and has a good surface for drawing, painting or inking.

Whatever is contained within the camera-ready artwork will be faithfully reproduced by the camera. So any slips and mistakes on the artwork will be carried through the other stages in the production chain. In order to get a satisfactory end result, you must therefore observe some simple rules imposed by the very nature of printing.

1. *Cleanliness:* Your hands and the surface that you are working on *must* be clean. This also applies to the table, any other surrounding objects, and the drawing equipment – pens, pencils, brushes, rulers, T-squares, erasers, and so on.

2. *Squareness:* The printing press is designed to handle sheets of paper which are cut square; that is, all their corners are right angles. Your artwork must relate to this squareness. If you want even margins all round and the text and illustrations to be aligned, then your work has to be as accurately 'squared up' as the paper is (see pasting up, page 122). The human eye has an uncanny ability to detect small imperfections in squareness, and the odd line or word that is not at right angles to other parts of the image or the edge of the paper stands out. Unfortunately, like other errors, they are more obvious when printed than on the artwork. (Before sending finished artwork to the printer, it is a good idea to photocopy it, and check the alignment and other design features on the photocopy – it often reveals mistakes which are quite difficult to see on the actual artwork.)

3. *Evenness:* The density of the black on the artwork should be consistent. Artwork is always done in black, regardless of in what colour the item is to be printed. If the image is inconsistent – if parts of it are grey and not a true black – then the camera will record that part as a smudgy texture of fine black specks, and the printed item will be unsatisfactory. So remember, if you are pasting down lettering, type, or an illustration or photograph, make sure that the tone of each image is consistent.

4. *Edges:* The camera will pick up any dirty edges of the paper pasted to the baseboard. The printer can touch out any unwanted material on the film, but it is difficult and expensive. You can clean up dirty edges with an eraser or by rubbing gently with a piece of clean tissue or cotton soaked with a little solvent such as lighter fuel. Stubborn marks can be covered with white artists' paint or typists' correction fluid. Whichever method is used, take great care to avoid damaging the image you want to print.

Defining the page

Every piece of artwork must include guide marks to define the page area. All these marks – corner, registration and fold marks – are printed in the area that will be trimmed away.

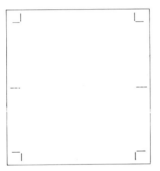

Corner marks
These marks should be made on the artwork and are printed. They act as guide lines for the blade of the trimming machine. Most artwork is printed on paper larger than the finished size and then trimmed. When trimmed, the corner marks disappear.

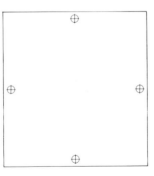

Registration marks
If the item being printed is prepared from two or more pieces of artwork (for instance, if it is printed in two colours and the artwork for each colour has been prepared separately), then registration marks are included on each separate piece of artwork. The camera photographs each piece, and the marks on each piece of film can be aligned for printing to ensure the correct positioning of one colour on top of another. You can make registration marks simply by drawing a cross with a fine pen; or alternatively you can use type available as a dry transfer, as in this diagram.

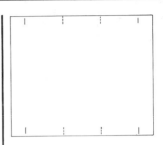

Fold marks
In addition to corner and registration marks, some items require folding. Fold lines are usually indicated by dotted lines drawn along the part of the paper or card which should be creased for folding.

Making the base artwork

All artwork should be drawn and pasted on to a good quality artboard or heavy paper. Ink lines drawn on cheap material tend to 'creep' along the board's fibres, giving a 'hairy' appearance to the lines. So buy the more expensive material which has a smooth hard surface.

Always use a sheet of board that is rather larger than the artwork area. This gives you room to 'see' the work properly and, possibly, to include any notes needed for the printer who will be converting your image on to film. The first thing to do is lightly pencil in the corner marks (carefully squared up with the edges of the board) and any fold marks that might be needed.

Then pencil in your grid (see chapter 7) or, if this is unnecessary, the boundaries within which you want any type or drawing to appear. Draw these lines in lightly, using a light blue pencil or crayon which will not be picked up by the camera.

Having established your position guides, you can now begin to paste down the required type, pictures, diagrams and lettering, using your design as a guide (see pasting up, page 122). This must be done carefully and accurately, otherwise you will lose the squareness and sense of 'quality' that the artwork should have. Certain types of multi-colour artwork are prepared in exactly the same way, using an overlay for each different colour required. The printer will make one film for each overlay (colour); the process is explained in more detail in chapter 10.

Pasting up

Collect the basic tools and materials required (see below) and any other pieces of equipment you may need such as dry transfer rules or borders, compass, French or flexible curves, and so on. Clear your work space of any unwanted items.

Assemble the elements to be pasted down. Remember that photographs are not usually pasted down unless you have already had screened photographic prints made to the correct size. (Screened photographs and line matter can be photographed together on the printer's camera – unscreened photographs have to be photographed separately even if they are already the correct size.)

When the job is completed, remember to check artwork for cleanliness and add a protective overlay. This should be made from tracing paper and stuck down on the reverse of the board to fold over the top edge. Instructions to the printer can be added to the overlay rather than to the margin of the artwork if this is clearer. It is useful to mark each piece of artwork so the printer can keep a check on it. A good idea is to say 'Item 2 of 3', and so on.

EQUIPMENT CHECKLIST

Assemble the tools and materials you need.

Basic tools:	Basic materials:
Drawing board with at least one square, flat edge	Artboard (for base of artwork), or smooth, coated paper
T-square	Masking tape (2.5 cm – 1 inch)
Set square	Cleaning spirit (lighter fuel or similar)
Ruler	
Steel rule	
Scalpel	Cotton wool or tissue
Light blue pencil (or hard lead pencil)	Several sheets clean white paper
Ruling pen (cartographers, draught or modern fine felt tip)	Adhesive – rubber, wax or spray

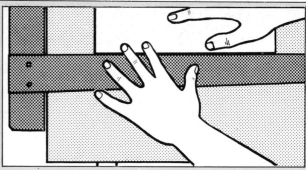

1. With a craft knife or scalpel, cut the material to be used for the artwork base to size – leaving at least a 5 cm (2 inch) border all around.
Square up the bottom edge of the board with the T-square. Keep the left-hand edge of the artboard near to the straight left-hand edge of the board. (Even with a new and well-made drawing board and T-square, the further away from the left-hand edge of the board the less accurate the squareness will be.) Use masking tape to secure the art board to the drawing board.

2. Draw up the guide lines for the paste-up in blue pencil. Position the whole image area squarely and in the centre of the art board. Then draw in the page border, the corner marks and the centre or folding marks. Draw in guide lines within the trim area. Reproduce accurately the grid you prepared when you did your initial design. If you only did a rough design, you must decide on the accurate positions now – but be prepared to try various spacings before you complete the job.

3. Now prepare each item to be pasted down: PMTs, photosetting and so on. Place pasted items onto a piece of card and trim artwork using a scalpel and straight edge. The separate pieces can then be picked up as needed.

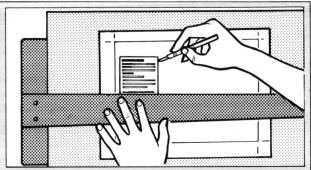

4. Pick up one of the larger pieces of typematter with the scalpel and place it gently in position on the grid. Move the T-square up across the typematter so that its edge is just below one of the longest lines. Then, still using the scalpel, steer the typematter so that the lines of type are horizontal. Move it sideways and up and down until it is exactly in position. Be careful that the T-square does not catch and lift pieces as it is moved about. Once the piece is in the correct position, cover it with a piece of clear blank paper and rub it down with firm, even pressure (small rubber rollers can be bought for this purpose).

5. Continue to assemble the items. Very small pieces (for instance, a page number) should be stuck down using **double-sided tape rather than adhesive. Unpeel a piece of tape and stick it to** the back of the sheet carrying the item to be pasted down. Then stick the sheet down on to a firm surface. Carefully cut around the item through to, but not into, the tape's backing material. Peel it off the backing material on the scalpel point and place in position on paste-up. Once all the items have been pasted down, remove any traces of adhesive and trim any backing paper that is curling or overlapping onto another piece. Ensure that all items are stuck firmly and cleanly.

6. Now draw in rules and borders (using a ruling pen or dry transfer tape), and ink in the corner marks, centre marks and any other marks for the printer. Using a blue or lead pencil draw in the shape and position of any items such as photographs which are to be positioned by the printer. These must be labelled and keyed in.

Overlays

The overlay is a sheet of material, usually transparent, which is used to cover and protect original artwork, and to carry written instructions for the printer. It is also used in the preparation of multi-colour artwork, where parts of the image must be separated because they will be printed in different colours; and sometimes in single-colour printing (when, for example, a map showing physical features is going to be repeated several times, while the annotation on each map is different).

Materials for overlays

Tracing paper, plastic film or acetate can be used for overlays, although they each have advantages and disadvantages:

Tracing paper: This is cheap and transparent enough for most positioning purposes. If you only wish to draw pen lines on it, or lay dry transfers down on it, tracing paper is adequate. But if you wish to use large areas of paint or ink, then it is liable to wrinkle and distort the image.

Plastic overlay film (such as Kodatrace): A plastic sheet, semi-transparent and with a matt finish. It is also 'dimensionally stable', that is, it does not wrinkle when liquid paint or ink is put on it. It is very easy to work with, but is expensive.

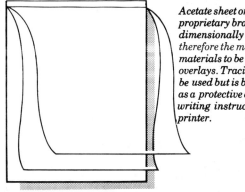

Acetate sheet or similar proprietary brands are dimensionally stable and are therefore the most suitable materials to be used for overlays. Tracing paper can be used but is best used just as a protective cover for writing instructions to the printer.

Acetate: This is a completely transparent plastic sheet, which enables you to see the exact relationship – not just the position, but also the appearance – between what is on the overlay and what is on the baseboard. Dimensionally stable, but not as easy to draw on as plastic film.

When preparing artwork which will be printed in two colours, the design may call for them to overprint in some areas. In this case, it is much easier to prepare the images for each colour separately. The printer will simply produce one film for the base and one for the overlay.

The overlay is usually attached to the baseboard by folding it over the top edge and taping it to the back of the board so that it can be lifted easily to reveal the image below. To ensure that the overlay and the base are kept in the correct relative positions, registration marks are used. These should be placed on the base artwork just outside the trimmed area. The overlay can then be attached to the baseboard and the registration marks traced through.

Type reversal

Letters which appear white on a dark background instead of black on a light background have been through a process called 'reversal' (often referred to as 'white out of black'). The same effect could be achieved, of course, by using white paint, or white dry transfer lettering, on top of a dark printed image, but a more professional effect is achieved by producing the letters in black on an overlay, and positioning that accurately over the base artwork. The printer will then reverse the lettering by photographic means.

This also applies to anything else you wish to appear in white: an illustration or a diagram, for example. It is easier to draw a fine diagram in black ink on a white background than in white ink on black.

Combining type with pictures

Sometimes you will wish to place type over a photograph. If your photograph has large, pale areas, then you can impose black type over these areas. But if the photograph is predominantly dark, white type will be more readable. In either case do not draw or lay down transfer letters on top of the actual photograph. If you have stuck down the photograph on the base artwork you can prepare the lettering on an overlay and then position it over the photograph. The printer will then combine the two photographically. However, photographs are not usually pasted down on the base artwork. An accurate outline (called a *keyline*) of the photograph or illustration, which indicates just where it is to go, should be drawn on

You may wish to print type in black over pale areas of an illustration such as a photograph.
Alternatively you may wish to reverse type white out of a dark area. Do not try to add lettering directly to the illustration but place on an overlay above it in the correct position (right). The printer will then combine them photographically.

to the artwork, and then any type or lettering positioned accurately on an overlay or on the base artwork itself.

Producing two-colour artwork: simple colour separation

When producing artwork to be printed in more than one colour, the printer must make a separate litho plate, block, or silk screen for each colour to be printed. This is made simpler if the artwork for each colour is 'separated', that is, mounted on different overlays.

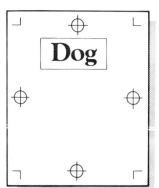

1. Prepare the baseboard: clean it, note the crop marks, and place registration marks on four sides of the board outside the area to be printed. Indicate any grid lines or positioning marks in light blue pencil, then paste up all the elements of the design which print black (or the colour which is being used for the major part of the design).

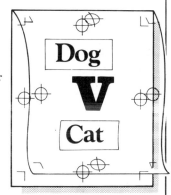

2. Position an overlay over the baseboard, and clean it with a solvent such as lighter fuel (unless the overlay is made of tracing paper, in which case just dust it). Position the corner and registration marks in *exactly* the same place on the overlay as they occur on the baseboard. Position all the elements to be printed in the second colour on the overlay. Repeat step 2 for each colour included in your design.

The same technique can be used to introduce colour into black and white line illustrations. Usually the detail of the illustration is printed in black, and blocks of colour are added in various areas to give a more exciting effect.

1. Paste down the illustration on the base artwork and position an overlay over it.

2. Trace the outlines of the areas where the second colour should fall from the base artwork on to the overlay.

3. Once the outlines are drawn in, fill in the areas with ink.

This technique can be used to particularly good effect in diagrams.

To vary the range of colour, the printer can use a tint of the colour instead of the solid colour; the overlay is drawn in exactly the same way as for solid colour.

Marking up for the printer

There are three elements for which you must provide specific instructions for the printer or typesetter. These are the copy, the illustrations and the base artwork.

Preparing copy for typesetting

Ensure that the manuscript (ms) or copy has been thoroughly checked and rechecked for spelling, punctuation, and uniformity of style. The typesetter will correct his or her own mistakes free, but yours (author's corrections) will be charged for and are expensive.

Copy should be typed double spaced on one side of the paper, leaving wide margins either side and at the top and bottom for instructions and corrections. If you are giving the typesetter more than one sheet, number and indicate on each how many pages in all; for example, page 2 of 10. Title each sheet, and keep a copy of everything you give him.

Mark corrections in ink or another permanent medium above the line they relate to. Try not to use the side margins too much, and avoid attaching odd pieces of paper with corrections.

Type mark-up

The following information will be needed by typesetters for *every* item you ask them to do, even if it is just a few lines. Mark up the copy in a coloured pen to distinguish it from the typed manuscript.

1. *Typeface*, and the variation or member of family. For example, Helvetica (typeface) medium (variation). If more than one member of a family of type or other faces are being used, indicate which is to be used where.

2. *Type size*.

3. *Line spacing*, measured in points. The type size and the line spacing are often specified together; for example, 10 point type with 1 point leading is indicated as '10 on 11 point' (or '10/11 pt'). Use this method of expressing type size and leading only if the leading is between ½ and 2 points; beyond that say '10 point with 3 point leading'.

4. *Line length*. If the copy is likely to run on beyond one line – for example, if it is a long title or a block of text – you must specify how wide each line is to be, and whether they are to be centred, range left, range right or justified.

5. *Indentation*. Indicate if any line, such as the first line of a paragraph, should start further in than the rest and by how much.

6. *Spacing*. Apart from line spacing you may want to indicate space between a title and a block of text, or space for an illustration. This can be done either in type measurement (points) or in conventional measures.

7. *Capitalization*. Ensure that capitalized letters and other variations – for example, italics, bold type, and so on – are indicated with proof readers' marks.

This piece of copy has been marked up for the typesetter. The type specification includes the typeface, type size, line spacing and line length, and editorial corrections have been made using proof-readers' marks.

MARKING UP COPY FOR THE TYPESETTER		
Mark in text	*Mark in margin*	*Instruction to typesetter*
ʎ	ʎ	Insert new material
/	ᵒ͡	Delete
⌇⌇⌇	Bold	Bold
___	Italic	Italic
═══	sc	Make small capital letters
≡≡≡	cops	Change to capital letters
⌐⌐	run on	Run on
Word⌐first	trs	Transpose
⌐Word	⌐┘	Move to right
⌐Word	└─	Move to left
To or ⓉⓄ	lc	Change to lower case
⌐┘	np	New paragraph
ʎ	#	Insert space
·····	stet	Leave as printed or typed

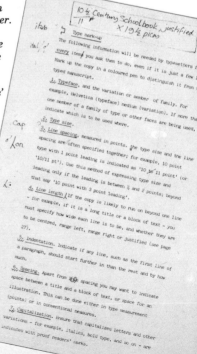

Marking up illustrations

The printer or origination house will need the following information.

1. *Position of illustrations in layout.* Although often separate from the base artwork, they must be keyed into it. If the instructions or the base artwork say 'Photograph A here', for instance, the photograph must be marked 'A' (on an overlay).

2. *Final size.* Dimension lines should be accurately drawn and labelled on the illustration's overlay. If it requires no enlargement or reduction, mark it 'same size' or 's/s'.

3. *The area of the photograph to be used.* Trace this on to the overlay. The area(s) to be deleted are usually scribbled out to show they are unwanted.

4. *Special instructions.* Most illustrations are rectangular in shape – or 'squared-up' in printers' terminology – and this is implied if no other instruction is given. If you want to retain only an irregularly shaped portion of an illustration, this is called a 'cut-out'. The area to be removed is clearly traced and scribbled over on an overlay, and the instruction 'cut-out' should be clearly written over the remainder.

5. *Printing instructions.* For example, in which colours (if more than one), and whether as a line illustration or a halftone. If the illustration is to be printed as a halftone, indicate the coarseness or fineness of screen (see pages 134-5), or the type of screen if a special style is required. If it is to be printed in two or more colours, you must specify whether you require it to be printed as a duotone (see page 136) or a four-colour process (see page 137).

Marking up the artwork

The overall size of the finished item should be specified on every piece of artwork and the dimension lines indicated, even if the artwork is exactly the finished size you want. Label the trim, centre and registration marks, and indicate whether they are to be deleted after use.

If the artwork has an overlay, ensure that it is correctly positioned and that its register marks coincide with those on the base. Check that there are full instructions indicating how the material on the overlay should be dealt with; for example, which colour it is to be printed in, and how it should integrate with the base artwork.

If spaces are left for other artwork, ensure that everything is keyed in clearly. Positioning information must also be given; for example, pencil in the basic outline of an illustration. If an illustration is to sit in a box which has been drawn in on the artwork, ensure that the instructions indicate that the box is not just a guide to position, but that it is to be retained.

Instructions to the printer can either be written on the artwork (outside the print area), or on an overlay attached to it. In addition, written instructions should be provided on a separate piece of paper.

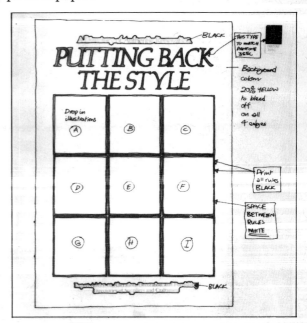

10. PRINTING AND COPYING METHODS

The choice of a particular printing or copying method depends on the following factors:
1. How many copies or prints are needed.
2. How much money is available.
3. When the job has to be finished.
4. What sort of print quality is wanted.

Each printing and copying method has its advantages, limitations and uses. The quality of a printed item usually depends on how much it costs, and the more colours used the more expensive it gets. When pressed for time a photocopying machine would be the quickest method, but a main street print shop can often produce things in a few hours. Print processes are more expensive than copying methods such as carbon paper or photocopying, but give you better results. So you may have to compromise between what you can afford and what you would like.

Copying methods

Carbon paper
Carbon paper is available in black, blue and red. To make a copy, a sheet is placed, carbon side down, between two pieces of paper. The pressure on the top sheet of paper as you write or type transfers carbon on to the sheet underneath. The pressure of typewriter keys is usually enough to make the original and three carbon copies.

Carbon-impregnated paper
This works on a similar principle to carbon paper, except that it is the copy paper which contains the carbon. When you place a piece of carbon-impregnated paper underneath the top sheet anything you write or type is also recorded on the

Carbon-impregnated paper is easier and less messy to use than carbon paper. It works on the same principle, but it is the copy paper which is impregnated with carbon.

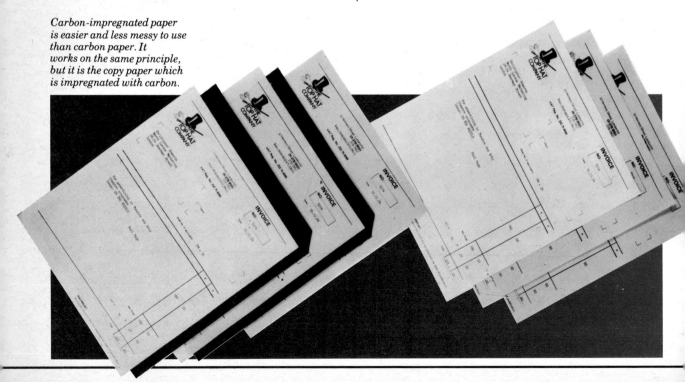

copy. Up to six copies can be made at one time. The most common use of this type of paper is for invoices and receipts where both the customer and the company can keep a copy. The paper can also be used to print on.

Rubber stamps

Rubber stamps are used for small symbols or messages which are used repeatedly, but which for some reason are not printed on the object. For example, a new telephone number would be stamped on to existing printed stationery, or reference details can be stamped on letters received. Some stamps can be bought ready-made; for example, a date stamp, which allows you to change the day, month and year.

A stampmaker will make a stamp with a message or symbol of your own choice; these can be ordered directly from a rubber stampmaker or through a print shop or stationer. If you provide the artwork, make sure the letters are big enough: for lower case letters do not use a type size less than 10 point; for capitals 9 point is adequate.

Ink stencil duplicating

This copying method, the forerunner of photocopying, involves a simple machine. The process is known under several names: the commonest are the mimeograph and the Gestetner. To make copies you write or type on to a sheet of special paper, which is porous and coated with a soft substance. The pressure from the pen or typewriter keys breaks the soft surface substance and exposes the porous paper beneath. This is then used like a stencil on the machine. Ink is forced through the porous paper only in those places where the pen or typewriter broke the surface. The machine can duplicate up to 1,000 copies in one run. However, removing the stencil and then reusing it weakens and shortens its life. These sort of ink stencil duplicators are widely used in schools to circulate information at minimum cost.

Rubber stamps have hundreds of applications. When designing them make sure that you do not make the letters too small.

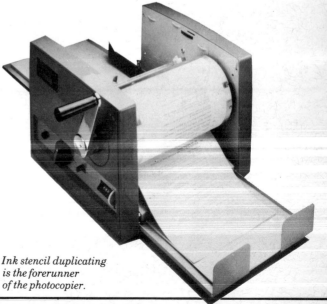

Ink stencil duplicating is the forerunner of the photocopier.

Photocopying

Photocopiers are also machines that duplicate an original. But they work in a very different way to the ink stencil duplicators. The material that is to be copied is placed face down on a glass plate and kept in position with a cover. When the machine is activated a light scans the original, making the copy paper underneath sensitive (electrostatically charged) in the places where black appears on the original. A resinous dust inside the machine is attracted to the sensitive areas. To adhere the dust to the page, the paper goes through metal rollers which are hot enough to melt the resin in the dust and fix the image.

The main limitation of most photocopying machines is that, although lines and large areas of black can be copied, the fine details are not

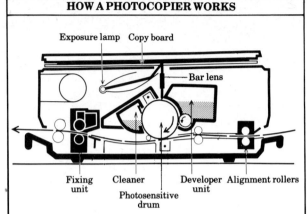

HOW A PHOTOCOPIER WORKS

Exposure lamp   Copy board

Bar lens

Fixing unit   Cleaner   Developer unit   Alignment rollers

Photosensitive drum

The electrostatic photocopier is now the most common type in use. It uses a dry process, copies on almost any material and now develops few copying faults. The copy is placed face down on the copy board, is scanned and the image transferred to the photosensitive drum. The developer or toner adheres to the image on the drum, which is transferred to the paper. The image is then fixed on to the paper by heat and pressure. The photocopier is an invaluable tool for a designer. Not only can it be used for ordinary document copying and as a short run printing machine, it is also useful for visualizing, preparing artwork and proofing. A visual can be partly or completely constructed of photocopied elements which can be cut up and coloured. High quality photocopiers will sometimes produce copies good enough to use as artwork. Also, artwork is easily proofed with a photocopier, giving you an opportunity to check for errors otherwise missed. Modern machines can copy on white and coloured paper, tracing paper and acetate sheet. Some can reduce and enlarge the original, and colour photocopiers are now available although they only use a limited range of coloured tones.

reproduced. Compare the photocopy below right with the original; all the grey tones in the photograph were too fine to be picked up by the machine.

What you can do with a photocopier
Photocopying machines have become more sophisticated. Although they still work on the same basic principle, new facilities have been developed. Some photocopying machines can reduce or enlarge the original. This enables you to reduce or enlarge a given number of words or illustrations so that they can be fitted into a smaller or larger space.

Most machines can now take different sorts of paper. This means you could use a coloured paper (use light coloured paper so the black shows up well). 'Iron-on' paper, used for ironing transfers on to T-shirts or similar fabrics, can be used in some machines. (If you want to make an iron-on transfer, do not forget to design the original in reverse so that the words and images are the right way round when they are transferred on to cloth.)

Colour photocopiers can make colour copies from photographs and slides, although the quality is usually poor.

Where to use a photocopier
Most quick print shops and office suppliers have photocopying machines that you can use or that will be operated for you. You pay by the copy. There are usually machines in libraries, too, which are available for public use. If the result is grey and smudged find another machine. If you have been shown a good photocopy, but the ones you receive look grey and smudged, then refuse to pay for them.

There are usually several paper sizes to choose from. If you want more than 100 copies, it would probably be cheaper to use a printing method. Ask a printer to estimate a price before you decide which method would be best.

PHOTOCOPYING

Printing methods

Letterpress

Letterpress is one of the oldest printing methods. Pressure is used to transfer the ink from a raised area of the printing plate directly on to the surface to be printed. A potato cut works on the same principle.

The platemaker transfers a reverse image of the words and pictures on the artwork on to the plate photographically. Acid is used to eat away the unwanted area surrounding the image, so that the area to be printed stands out in relief.

The metal plate is then placed on the printing press and ink is rolled over its surface: the non-image area, being lower, does not receive any ink (and therefore does not print). The paper is then rolled over the plate and the ink from the raised surface is impressed on the paper.

Letterpress was once used for everything, from newspapers to packaging. It is still used on a small scale: you may find a local printer who uses a small letterpress to print handbills and invitations. But the process has been superseded by lithography, which is generally quicker and more versatile.

Lithography

Lithography is based on the principle that water and oil do not mix. The image area on a lithographic plate – which is inked and dampened for each impression – is treated with a greasy medium to attract oil-based ink, while the non-image area is dampened with water, which repels it. When paper is lightly rolled across the plate, the inked image is transferred on to it.

Offset lithography is the commercial development of lithography, which is mainly reserved for fine art. Offset lithography works on the same principle, but the plate does not touch the paper. Instead the printing plate comes into contact with the dampened rubber rollers, which

The four basic printing processes shown in simplified form. From left to right, they are stencil (silk screen), in which the stencil is attached to a fine screen and the ink forced through the open areas; planographic (lithography), where a solution of water, gum arabic and acid on the printing plate attracts and holds the lithographic ink, which is then transferred on to the paper;

intaglio (gravure), in which ink collects in the hollows of the plate or block and is transferred onto the paper; and relief (letterpress), where only the raised areas of the plate are inked and have contact with the paper.

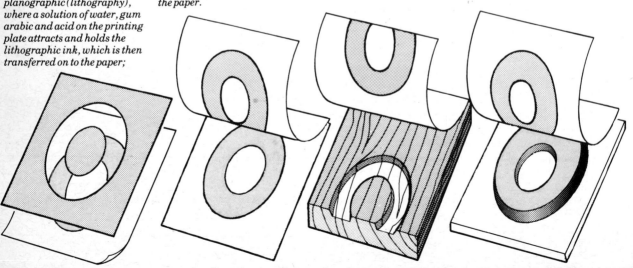

wet the plate with a solution of water, gum arabic and acid. The non-image area accepts this water solution, while the image area rejects it. Then the plate is inked: the image area accepts the ink; the water solution repels it in the non-image area. The inked image is then 'offset' on to a cylinder, which transfers the image to the paper.

The lithographic plate

The printer requires artwork for anything which is to be printed by lithography. This artwork is the original from which the plate will be made.

To make the plate, the artwork is photographed and the film negative is placed in front of the metal plate, which has been made sensitive to light. Light is shone through the film on to the plate: the image on the film is transferred to the plate, which is then chemically treated so that the image area will accept ink and reject the water solution, and the non-image area will reject the ink and accept the water solution.

For each colour to be printed, a separate plate – and therefore a separate piece of artwork – is needed. Usually the artwork is made up in black, because the film used to photograph it is sensitive to black; but the item is printed with the colour that you specify. Full-colour artwork is only used when it itself is to be reproduced – as in the case of making prints from a painting.

If you cut out a photograph from a magazine or book to use in your artwork it will probably look very coarse when printed: this is because it already has a dot screen over it. It is preferable to use an original photograph, but if you have to use a magazine photograph ask the printer to try and avoid screen clash.

Words and line drawings look better if reproduced by line film, while tone film should be used for photographs. The platemaker 'strips' (combines and fits) one with the other if necessary. Using two different types of film is a little more expensive than using only one, but produces a better quality result.

Screenprinting

Screenprinting is used to print words and pictures on a multitude of surfaces. Printed tins and road signs are likely to have been screen-printed. For large bold, brightly coloured posters using large areas of colour, screenprinting is probably the best method. And a wide variety of surfaces – metal, wood, ceramic, gloss, plastic, fabric, cardboard and paper, for example – are suitable for this process. It has the added advantage of being relatively inexpensive.

In screenprinting, ink is pushed through a screen of very fine material on to paper. The areas of the screen not required for an image are masked out with a stencil or gum, and the ink is then forced through the uncovered (image) area on to the surface to be printed.

It is easy to make and use a screenprinting process at home (see page 138), using a stencil made from paper or plastic. The process is also used commercially. When a printer uses the screen process, the image is transferred to the screen photographically.

The most important advantage of screenprinting is that solid colour can be printed with opaque ink: this means you can print one colour over another; for example, white type can be printed on black paper. Because of this it is a particularly popular method for printing over brightly coloured paper or fabric, and is generally used for items such as posters or T-shirts. Screenprinting also allows you to use shiny inks on a matt paper, while other processes are dependent on the paper to give a shiny effect.

Because of the structure of the screen, screenprinting is a coarser method of printing than lithography, which can achieve very delicate effects. With screenprinting, you should avoid lines thinner than 0.5 mm ($\frac{1}{32}$ inch), and type smaller than 9 point Roman medium (9 point light will be too thin).

Artwork for screenprinting is prepared in the same way as for all the other processes.

REPRODUCING THE IMAGE

Halftones

An ink drawing with a consistent density of blackness can be photographed and reproduced on line film just like the lettering and type that go alongside it. Printers call both *line work;* any image that is either black or white falls into this category.

lines, dots and cross-hatching. Because they are very fine, from a distance the eye does not see them as separate lines, but 'adds them up' with the white background and sees a 'grey'.

Continuous tone cannot be reproduced by printing varying strengths of ink. Instead, photographs are printed using the halftone screen. The illustration reproduced in halftone works in the same way as the engraving: by fooling the human

A photographic print has continuous tone – smooth changes of black through grey to white.

Line reproduction has no greys – light areas become white and dark areas black.

A continuous tone photograph has to be printed using a halftone screen (see enlargement below).

A moire pattern is caused if a screened halftone photograph is screened again for printing.

But if the drawing consists of various shades of grey, as well as black and white, then it does not have tonal consistency. If the printer photographed an illustration containing areas of grey in the same way as line work, the image on the film would break down into odd shaped blotches of black and white. Instead of the smooth changes of black through greys to white (known as *continuous tone*), there would be only either black or white; detail would be lost and it might be difficult to identify the original illustration.

An engraving appears, at first glimpse, to have areas of grey in it. But if you look closely you will see that those 'grey' areas are actually fine

eye. In this case, a tiny dot of black ink on a white background is seen by the eye as grey. The area of black, compared with the area of white, determines the depth of grey.

For a halftone, the printer photographs the original as for line work. But a slightly more sensitive film called tone film is used, on which a special screen is placed between the original and the film. On the screen is a finely ruled grid pattern; usually the rules are as wide as the gaps between them.

The screen reduces the original photograph to a vast number of small dots. These dots will vary in size, shape and number, depending on the tonal area they represent. During photography, the image projected by the lens passes through the grid pattern of the screen to produce the required series of dots on the printer's film. The size of the dot is determined by the amount of light (amount of white) in the illustration.

By using different screens it is possible to alter the density of the pattern. In a newspaper photograph the dots are much further apart than they are in a high quality magazine: the screen is coarser. The newspaper is printed on rough paper using thin inks, and on presses built for speed rather than quality: closely spaced dots (fine screen) either would not print or would run together, losing the illusion of continuous tone.

The coarseness of a screen on tone film is measured in lines per centimetre (or inch). The coarse screens used for newspapers have between 65 and 85 lines per 2.5 cm (1 inch). Ordinary quality commercial work uses screens with 120 to 133 lines per 2.5 cm (1 inch); high-quality printing, especially in full-colour work, uses 133 to 200 lines. You should not need to specify the coarseness of the screen; the printer will decide what is most suitable.

Cut-out halftones
Most photographs are rectangular (or 'squared-up') in shape. However, they can be printed in non-square forms. This is done by simply painting out, in white, those parts of the original which are not to be reproduced; or by painting a white line around the parts to be reproduced and then cutting a paper mask to cover the rest of the blanked-out area. Alternatively, there are photographic means of achieving this result: you can instruct the printer to cut out parts of the original.

An example of a cut-out halftone.

Other applications of the halftone screen
Black and white halftones can be used in combination with flat blocks of colour (that is, blocks with a consistent size of dot throughout), to give added impact to your pictures. But it is important not to use too dark a colour or the photograph will not be clearly visible: it is better to use a *tint,* or screen, of colour rather than a solid colour. This tint is itself a series of fine dots, but of unvarying density, which gives a paler version of the colour chosen: usually 20 per cent, 40 per cent or 80 per cent of the original colour density.

Blocks of tint or screen can be used as a design feature. For instance, a block of grey, achieved by printing a flat screen of black, can be used to vary appearance when using one or two colours only.

The tint can be made by the printer photographically or by using a ready-made dry transfer version; the photographic version has a higher quality. To prepare the artwork, just draw the outline of the area to be covered by the tint in black ink on an overlay – the printer will do the rest. (Areas of solid colour – no dots – are specified in the same way.)

Duotones

The duotone works on the same principle as the halftone, but in a slightly more sophisticated way: two colours are used, giving added depth and richness to an image.

A halftone will usually lose a little of the original photograph's detail in the very dark and very light areas, although it represents the greys quite well. Photographically, the printer can adjust the camera to concentrate either on the dark (shadow) areas and greys (middle tones), or on the light (highlight) and greys: the other tones will not be completely ignored, but will not be represented so well. The duotone compensates for this tonal imbalance.

To make a duotone, the printer makes two negatives of the same photograph; one concentrating on the shadow and middle tones, and the other on the highlight and middle tones. These are used to print the subject in two colours.

1. This image has been separated into dots for reproduction in one colour.
2. The same image, when treated for reproduction as a

duotone, is broken down into areas of dots twice: once with a bias towards the dark areas, and once with a bias towards the light (**shown enlarged**).

3. A print (in black) of one of the two negatives, showing the bias towards dark areas.

4. A print (in black) of the other negative, showing the bias towards light areas.

5. The image printed as a duotone, with the dark areas printing black and the light areas printing in the second colour.

6. The image printed again as a duotone, this time with the dark areas printing in the second colour, and the light areas in black.

The four-colour process

The four-colour process of reproducing full-colour artwork or photographs is similar to that of reproducing a black and white image: the image is comprised of dots. However, the image is converted from continuous tone to a number of dots four times, rather than once. The four-colours employed (in fact, really three – magenta, cyan and yellow – the fourth is black, which gives detail, shadow and sharpness) are the minimum number that can be used to get a full-colour effect.

How it works

The image is photographed four times, each with a different colour filter which picks up one of four colours in the original. By this process the image is broken down four times into areas of dots, each corresponding to the density of one of the four colours.

On the left is an enlargement of the four colour example shown below which shows the arrangement of dots.

Each of these images is then printed one on top of the other. This combination of dots printed in the four colours gives the impression of continuous areas of differing colour.

Most full-colour separation is done by machines called scanners. These are computer-controlled, and use lasers to scan the image. The machines are able to make quite extreme changes in the colour balance of the original. Often a colour photograph of poor quality can be improved by the process, although this cannot be relied upon. The advent of the scanner has also reduced the cost of full-colour separation.

It is usual for the printer to supply proofs of full-colour work. This usually means making printing plates and running a small number of copies on a proofing press. The printer will often provide not only colour proofs, but proofs of each of the four colours, in various combinations. These are called *progressives*: the combination of colours is yellow, blue, red, black; then yellow and blue; yellow, blue and red, then all four colours together. Progressives can show why a reproduction is not correctly colour balanced.

The colours used to make up the image

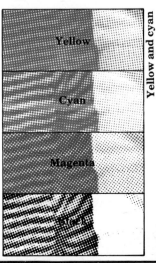

Yellow

Cyan

Magenta

Black

Yellow and cyan

Yellow and cyan and magenta

Four colour

Printing at home

Screen Printing
Making a frame
The framework for a screen should be simple, but of sturdy construction. Use wood not less than 5 × 5 cm (2 × 2 inches) and construct a frame slightly larger than the largest size you wish to print – at least 10 cm (4 inches) both horizontally and vertically. The four joints of the screen should be dovetailed together and glued with a strong wood adhesive. Ensure that all four corners are perfectly square.

The screen must be hinged and secured to the table or surface on which you are proposing to print, so that you may lift the screen and support it while you remove a freshly printed piece of paper. If you do not wish to fix your screen permanently, hinge it to a block, which can be G-clamped to the printing table or surface.

The hinges attaching the screen to the fixed anchor *must* be open ended to enable you to remove the screen easily for cleaning.

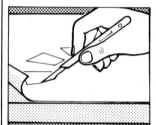

Stretching the screen
Lay a piece of nylon mesh over the frame, ensuring that it is 4 cm (1½ inches) larger than the screen all round.
Secure the nylon screen to the frame with staples, gently pulling the material taut, and stapling in the order shown in the illustration.
Again repeat this sequence, halving the distance between each staple, until you have gone round the screen leaving about 2.5 to 4 cm (1 to 1½ inches) between each staple. The screen should be tight, with an even pressure over the entire surface. When pushed very hard it should give no more than 7.5 cm (3 inches) in the centre.

Making Stencils
Hand-cut stencils can be made from low-grade paper, such as newsprint. The stencil is attached to the underside of the screen with masking tape. Although cheap, the paper stencil has a comparatively short life, and is not suitable for long runs.

To make a paper stencil, simply draw out your design on newsprint, cut out the areas you wish printed, and discard them. Then attach the stencil to the underside of the silk screen with masking tape.

Water-based stencils are made of a water-soluble film mounted on a thin sheet of acetate, and are suitable for long runs.

To prepare one, first place the sheet of stencil over a tracing of your design. With a sharp scalpel, cut around the areas to be printed. Then peel away the shapes from the backing material and discard them, leaving the stencil over those areas you do *not* wish to print.
To attach the stencil to the screen, press it, film side down, onto the underside of the screen and dampen both with a wet cloth. When the water has dried, carefully peel the backing sheet away. The stencil will have adhered to the screen. Once the stencil is firmly attached, prepare the screen by lining the inside of it with gumstrip to prevent leakage of ink from between the stencil edge and the frame edge.

Printing

Having prepared the screen with the stencil, you must mark where the pieces of paper, or other material to be printed, are to be placed beneath the screen. This is done by taping four card markers on to your working surface as positioning guides.

How it works

In screenprinting, the ink on the screen is forced through the holes in the stencil (which is attached to the underside of the screen) by a squeegee. The squeegee is a piece of wood with a stiff rubber blade attached to one edge.
The rubber blade is placed downward in the ink and then swiftly and firmly pulled towards you. As it passes over the screen the ink is pushed through the screen on to the surface being printed. To prevent the screen from sticking to the paper or other

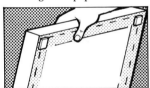

printing surface, it is raised slightly so that only the part of the screen being depressed by the squeegee is actually in contact with the surface at any one time. The necessary tension is provided by securing spacers of about 6 mm (¼ inch) in depth to the underside of the screen. These can be made from pieces of thick card, say 2.5 x 5 cm (1 x 2 inches), taped in position at each corner of the screen.
To make (or 'pull') a print, you will need the paper or other printing material plus some newspaper.

1. Place a sheet of newspaper against the spacer beneath the screen. Then lower the screen. Pour ink into the far edge of the screen so that it spreads to a band about 5 cm (2 inches) wide, and extends 5 cm (2 inches) or so either side of the area to be printed.

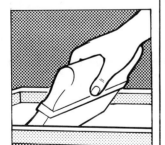

2. Place the squeegee, blade downwards, in the ink and angle it to 45 degrees towards you. Firmly and quickly pull the squeegee towards you, maintaining a constant downward pressure, and keeping the squeegee at 45 degrees.

3. Bring the squeegee to rest at the near edge of the screen, where there should be a second trough of ink – the residue which has not been forced through the screen. Lift up one end of the screen carefully and

4. Still keeping the squeegee at an angle of 45 degrees, push the trough of ink at the near end of the screen back over the stencil to the far end. This will make the area through which the ink is forced opaque with ink. It is essential that the opaqueness is even over the entire area to be printed. The screen has now been loaded with ink, and you can begin printing.

support it; remove the piece of newsprint and replace with the material on which you want to print. (Ensure that the angle to which you tilt the screen does not cause the ink to run back over the stencil.)

If you want to print in two or more colours, cut a new stencil for the application of each new colour and apply them, one by one, in the same way. But make sure that any existing colours are completely dry before you apply others.

Screen printing is a skilful process; one that needs practice. It is not difficult to acquire the knack, but do not be disheartened if your first efforts are not successful. Given time and practice you will see that it can be a clean, inexpensive and rewarding way of printing.

Cleaning the screen

When you have finished printing, scrape any excess ink off the screen and pour it back into the mixing pot. Most screen ink, once mixed with the appropriate thinners, will keep for some days. Never pour thinned ink back into a pot containing unthinned ink.

If you have been using paper stencils remove these. Then use the squeegee to force any remaining ink through the screen on to newspaper, in the same way you would when printing. Place some fresh newspaper underneath the screen and, with white spirit poured on to a rag, clean off any ink left on the screen.

You will need to repeat this process a number of times. Hold the screen up to the light so that you can see when it is clean. As long as it has been properly cleaned, the stained nylon fibres will not adversely affect any subsequent colour printed through the same screen.

Lino cuts

Lino cut prints are a simple and easy way of reproducing many copies of the same image. You need a piece of lino, a lino-cutting knife, two rollers, ink and paper and an inking surface (a small sheet of glass or metal is suitable).

EQUIPMENT CHECKLIST

Handle and lino cutters
Small sheet of glass
Two rollers
Ink

1. Draw your design on the piece of lino in pencil. Remember that the image on the lino is a 'mirror' or reverse image; so if you are including words they must be written backwards. Remove all the areas *not* to be printed with a cutting knife, taking care not to cut into the lino too deeply as this will weaken it. The areas to print should stand about 0.25 cm (⅛ inch) proud of the areas removed.

2. Having prepared the lino cut, ink the roller by smearing some ink on to the cleaned glass or metal surface and then pushing roller back and forth until the ink is evenly distributed on both the roller and the inking surface. Then run the roller back and forth across the prepared lino, until its surface is evenly covered with a thin layer of ink.

3. Place a sheet of paper on the inked lino, taking care not to knock it when it is in contact with the lino, as this will smudge the image. Firmly press the paper on to the lino by running a second (clean) roller back and forth a few times. Carefully peel the paper from the lino. Then re-ink the lino cut and repeat the process.

Rubber Lettering

This is available in a number of sizes – from those suitable for printing business cards to sets of letters large enough to be used on posters. Whatever the size, they work in exactly the same way, by inking the surface of the rubber letters and pressing them on to the surface you wish to print.

Letterpress machines

You can also buy small, manual letterpress machines. These usually only print a very small area – no more than postcard size. But they are ideal for printing business cards, invitations or change-of-address cards.

11. FINISHING AND PRESENTATION

Binding and Finishing

All printed material comes off the printing machine in flat sheets and, in most cases, the printed area has an unwanted margin around it. This is not normally the 'finished' object, unless you are producing a single, large, flat sheet such as a poster. In most cases, there are several stages to go through before the printed material becomes a finished object such as a booklet, a leaflet, or even stationery and cards.

Binding
The term binding covers the several operations involved in bringing together the printed sheets that make up any item of more than four pages – such as a leaflet, magazine or book – and securing them together. These are the operations usually performed in the binding process:
1. Each printed sheet is folded to form a signature.
2. The signatures are gathered together and collated in the correct order.
3. The collated signatures are then fastened together in one of several ways.
4. If necessary the three unfastened sides are trimmed to neaten the appearance.

Finishing
Finishing is a general term that covers a wide range of operations other than binding. Some are involved with box making and producing other three-dimensional items; some are designed to perform a protective function; and others are simply for decoration or to provide an alternative to printing the image.

There are a number of finishing techniques. The main ones are:
Die cutting: A method of punching out complex shapes using a metal-edged cutter. Usually done on letterpress machines.
Making-up and glueing: Assembling and glueing together. For example, attaching a strut (easel) to the rear of a showcard.
Mounting: Glueing a sheet on to a stronger backing, usually for display purposes.
Laminating: This usually refers to the covering of a printed surface with a glossy and transparent protective film of plastic, called film laminating.
Varnishing: A cheaper way of achieving almost the same effect as film laminating. A clear liquid is applied to the printed surface.
Embossing: A process that involves printing the image, then raising (or lowering) the same image. Usually seen on letterheads or decorative work. It is called blind embossing when ink is not used.
Die-stamping: Similar to embossing. An image is impressed on to the surface by a raised metal printing head called a die. The printer will make the die from your artwork. The design must be simple, with lines no thinner than 0.3 cm ($\frac{1}{8}$ inch).
Foil blocking: Similar to die-stamping. A heated metal block is used to make metal foil adhere to the printed surface. This process is often used on paperback book covers or on boxes.
Round cornering: Usually only a decorative effect. Can be done either during the die-cutting process, or, more cheaply, as a separate process using a tool like a chisel with a curved cutting edge.

If you are intending to do your own binding and finishing be sure that you do not underestimate the sheer slog involved. It is one thing to watch 250 sets of 20 pages spill out of a photocopying machine, it is another to collate them together, emboss the first page of each set, and then staple or even comb bind them with card covers!

You may not need to use any form of finishing or binding. A simple one- or two-sided leaflet which has a finished size the same as the sheet put through the photocopier or duplicator will not need any trimming. Formal invitations can be printed on ready-made blank cards with various finishes and decorative edges; for instance, wedding invitations can be printed on silver-edged cards. Deckle-edged cards can also be bought blank: these have edges that look as though they have been carefully torn, exposing the fibres of the board. (The effect can be simulated by careful tearing, providing you do not have too many to do.)

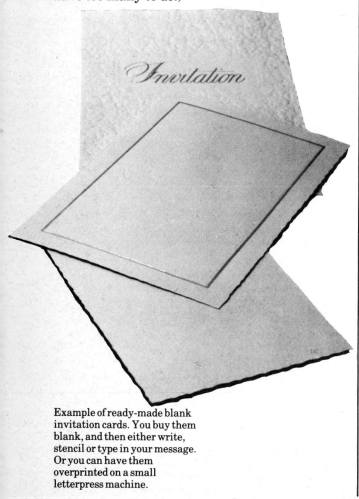

Example of ready-made blank invitation cards. You buy them blank, and then either write, stencil or type in your message. Or you can have them overprinted on a small letterpress machine.

Imposition

This is the arrangement of pages on a printed sheet which ensures that when the sheet is folded and signatures are collated they will be in the correct page order. The imposition of pages affects the printer, who has to ensure their correct arrangement when making plates. However, it is the binder who dictates how the pages will be imposed as it is his or her job to fold the sheet.

To make a simple four-page leaflet by folding a flat sheet once, the pages are numbered in the order they are read. To achieve this arrangement the printer will have to make two plates.

Alternatively, only one plate can be used.

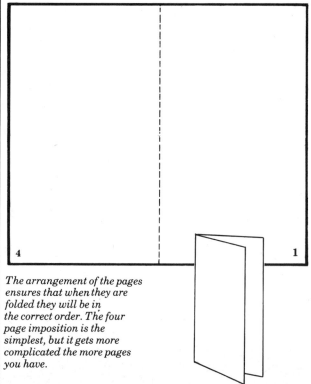

The arrangement of the pages ensures that when they are folded they will be in the correct order. The four page imposition is the simplest, but it gets more complicated the more pages you have.

With this arrangement the sheet is printed on one side, then turned over and printed from the same plate again so that pages 2 and 3 print on the back of 1 and 4, and vice versa. (This is sometimes called *work and turn.*) Of course, it makes two copies of the same material from one sheet.

When more than four pages are involved, imposition becomes more complicated. In addition to positioning pages in the correct order, it is also necessary to leave margins between some edges to allow for trimming after folding. When you are preparing artwork for this type of item, ask how the printer wants it presented. Usually, it will be in one- or two-page units. Sometimes the pages will be imposed before the artwork is converted to film or at film stage. Below is an example of one side of a 16-page signature. Because imposition determines which side of the printing sheet a page will fall it may also determine which pages are printed in which colours. For example, if you print one side of a sheet in one colour and the other in two colours, when folded, the colours will be interspersed with

each other. This gives the impression that two colours have been used throughout, and yet, on four pages, the cost of a second colour has been saved. (This saves on artwork, film, plates, machine time and ink.) If you intend to use colour in this way, discuss the imposition at the outset with your printer in order to achieve the maximum effect.

Folding

Folding can vary from bewilderingly complex machine operations to a very simple act carried out at home. The flat sheet comes off the folding machine as a group of pages, all in the correct order and folded: this is a *signature*. The page imposition for printing depends on the particular folding machine being used.

The most common commercial method of folding is to pass the sheet over a flat bed in which there is a long slot. Over the slot is a blade – not a cutting blade, but a blunt one – which pushes the paper down into the slot, then between a set of rollers. This folds the paper at precisely the right point. In order to obtain a 16-page signature, the sheet has to be folded three times by this method and the doubled page edges are automatically slit.

For a large book, there may be 20 or more separate 16-page signatures, which then have to be put into order and bound.

There are many other types of work which require more simple folding procedures, and

The most common method for high volume folding is to pass the paper over a slot in a flat bed. A blunt blade pushes the paper down into the slot, where rollers fold it in the precise point.

8	6	12	5
4	13	16	1

many of these are carried out by hand: a simple leaflet, for example, only requires one fold down its centre. With a little care and organization accurate folds can easily be achieved. A simple aid when folding paper in half is a thick straight edge: push one side of the paper flush against it, fold the paper over and butt the other side against the straight edge before making the crease.

Use a smooth blade-like or rod-like implement to sharpen the crease. Plastic rulers are excellent: they allow you to apply pressure, while moving the ruler flatly along the fold.

To fold paper in half, butt both edges up against a thick straight edge.

Scoring

To fold heavier material, such as board, score it first along the outside line of the fold; this breaks the fibres of the material so that a fold can be made neatly and easily. Scoring can be done on the printing machine if the board is not too heavy: a rule inserted into one of the cylinders of a litho press scores the printed sheet as it leaves the machine. But it is difficult to place the rule accurately, and generally printers prefer other methods. In the bindery, scoring can be done on foot- and hand-operated machines as a part of the folding process, again if the material is not too heavy. Often a letterpress machine is used to score very heavy board.

If you wish to fold board yourself, remember that the score must be on the outside of the fold.

Use a *blunt* edge to make the scoring indentation – it is important not to cut the board. The thicker the material the wider the scoring edge should be. If you are folding a cover for a thick booklet, you may have to make two folds.

Use a plastic ruler or other similar implement (left) to make a really sharp crease.

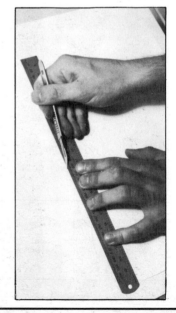

To fold heavier material such as board, first score with a blunt edge along the outside line of the fold. Do not use a sharp implement as it will cut the fibre of the board. The thicker the material the wider the scoring edge should be.

Trimming and cutting out

All printers have a paper cutter of some kind. Called guillotines, they vary enormously in their degree of automation and sophistication. Hand-operated office guillotines sometimes have an adjustable edge against which to position the material to be cut; or the baseboard may have a grid to help positioning. The most accurate and safest guillotine is the variety which incorporates a clamp to hold the material to be cut. All machines should have blade guards – any with open blades should be treated with the utmost caution.

Sharp blades are the safest: you will not need to apply so much pressure. Use light pressure and keep control *all* the time. Before making any cut, check that your fingers are nowhere near the

cutting line. Take care, too, when changing blades – observe the manufacturer's instructions.

Edge trimmers are useful for single-sheet trimming. These use a rotary head which slides along a bar mounted on one edge of the

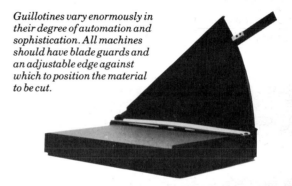

Guillotines vary enormously in their degree of automation and sophistication. All machines should have blade guards and an adjustable edge against which to position the material to be cut.

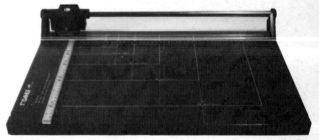

For cutting individual items there are a number of knives available. Scalpels and utility knives both have a range of blades for coping with different materials.
When using these knives, place a piece of board underneath the item you are cutting so that you do not cut the working surface.

baseboard. They cut paper, thin card, and other materials such as foil and acetate.

Obviously, printers handling large volumes of paper require something a little more powerful than a hand-operated guillotine. The printer's guillotine is a large knife blade, powered to cut large volumes of paper accurately. Many modern guillotines are electrically operated and can be pre-programmed to make a series of cuts to specific dimensions. They are extremely precise. Other guillotines have three or four cutting blades which are adjusted to trim to a set of dimensions; the blades work in series in order to do all the cutting required in one operation.

The guillotine is designed to cut precise straight lines at right angles to other straight lines. This means that no matter how often you cut the edges you will always end up with a square or a rectangle. Any shape more complicated than that will probably require a special blade, for which the printer will require a cutting guide to work from. This is a separate piece of artwork (usually an ink drawing) which shows the finished shape and dimensions.

From this guide a blade will be made corresponding to the finished shape. The printer may decide that the printed work has to be cut from one side rather than the other: find this out before you supply the cutting guide.

If you only have a small number of things to trim to size or cut shapes into, you will probably decide to do it yourself. To cut accurate straight lines safely you require a straight edge (preferably a metal one), a sharp craft knife, and an old piece of card to place under the work so that you do not cut the work surface.

Do not apply much pressure to the blade: the harder you press, the less control you will have and, in addition, the blade might snap under pressure. It is better to use several light controlled strokes rather than one heavy one. Always place the straight edge over the printed area rather than the unwanted margin, in case you slip or make a wrong cut.

Collation

The simplest way of collating pages in their order is to lay out a pile of page 1s, then next to it the page 2s, and so on around a large table. You can then walk around the table taking one page from each pile as you go. Ensure that all the pages are the right way up and the right way round. A little forward planning and an adequate amount of space is all that you really need.

Most modern collating machines are fully automated: they use jaws to extract pages from a series of boxes, and to place the pages on to a moving belt one on top of the other, in the correct order.

Large photocopying machines are fitted with sorting and collating bins. The copies are fed face down into individual bins as they come off the photocopying machine: each bin receives one page 1, one page 2 and so on. Obviously the number of copies is limited by the number of bins on the machine; but you can repeat the process as many times as is required.

When using a scalpel, beware of pressing too hard; the blade may snap and fly up towards your face. Always keep the edge against which you are cutting (a ruler or straight-edge) over the printed area to protect it in case the scalpel slips.

Three useful finishing techniques

Film laminating

Printers usually send film laminating work to a specialist. But you can film laminate an individual item by using adhesive-backed, transparent film, which is sold in rolls with a backing sheet. The technique for applying the film is the same as for any other adhesive film (see page 118).

Ensure the surface to be covered is flat and free from dust and grease. Lay the item to be laminated on the unrolled backed film and cut off a piece which is at least 1 cm (½ inch) larger all the way around. Peel off about 10 cm (4 inches) of backing paper across the full width and crease it. Position the exposed adhesive film along the top of the surface to be covered. Using a cloth, press down lightly and evenly, without distorting the film. Gently pull more of the backing paper away, evenly across the width, a little at a time, all the while smoothing the film down on to the surface with a cloth and working close to the receding backing paper. Avoid trapping air between the film and the surface. Any bubbles that do form can be pricked with a pin and smoothed down. Finally trim the excess film and paper away at the edges, taking care not to wrinkle the film.

Varnishing

Commercial varnishing, using a special preparation which is dried and cured by ultra-violet light, achieves a high gloss effect similar to film lamination, but at a lower cost. The varnishes available in aerosols which you can buy and use at home are really only a way of sealing the surface; they do not give a high gloss. But it would be sufficient for some items.

Making a showcard

To make a showcard stand up, a strut (easel) has to be made and attached to the back. It is often hinged so that it can be folded flat against the back when the card is not in use.

The strut can be cut from the same material as the showcard itself.

Binding

The amount of paper to be bound is a decisive factor in the choice of a binding method, which must be decided before the artwork is produced so that you leave the appropriate margins. Obviously, the binding must not obscure any of the page when the finished item is opened.

There are four main binding methods: stitching or sewing; mechanical binding; perfect binding; and edition binding.

Stitching and sewing

The paper is folded in one of several ways (see page 143) to make a signature. The signatures usually contain either eight, 16 or 32 pages (counting both sides of each sheet) and all the pages are folded down the spine as shown below.

The spine is either sewn or wire stitched to keep the pages together. The sewing method is more expensive than wire stitching but much neater. The sewn sections are usually no bigger than 32 pages: anything over this is too bulky.

Wire stitching is done by either saddle stitching or side stitching: loose pages can be bound with side stitching, but you need folded paper to do the saddle stitching.

Expense is one of the major factors when deciding what sort of binding you want, but basically the more expensive the system the longer the book or magazine will last.

Saddle stitching allows you to open the book or pamphlet flat and read it without having to hold the pages open. But the number of pages that the wire will bind successfully is limited and depends on the thickness of paper used. Most magazines are saddle stitched because it is efficient and cheap.

Side stitching is one of the cheapest binding methods. It, too, is done with wire, but the stitches are made at the side of loose pages, not folded ones. The stitches do tend to pull the book closed, so the reader has to hold it open: the thicker the book the more difficult it is to keep open.

Both kinds of wire stitching will last for about two years: eventually, either the wire rusts or the holes rip.

Mechanical binding

This is a little more expensive than wire stitching. There are several sorts of mechanical binding. They all work on the principle of punching holes into the paper and then threading wire or plastic through the holes to hold the pages together. The types of hole cut into the paper differ according to the method used; for example, the 'wire-o' binding technique uses slotted holes, while spiral binding method uses round ones.

Most mechanical binding needs more than

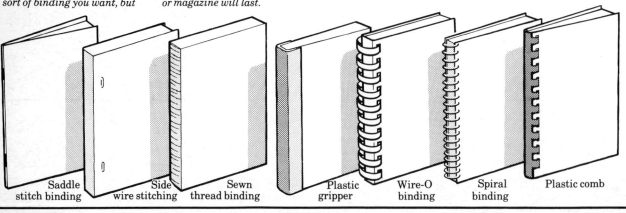

Saddle stitch binding Side wire stitching Sewn thread binding Plastic gripper Wire-O binding Spiral binding Plastic comb

the average space for the inside margin, so allow for this in your design.

Perfect binding

Perfect binding is the method used to bind most paperback books. All the sections of the book are cut with a guillotine so that the spine is smooth. The spine is then roughened to accept glue. After the glue is applied, the cover is creased and glued into position. The book is then trimmed so that

In pefect binding the spine is first trimmed and then roughened to accept glue.

The cover is then creased and glued into position.

Mostly used for paperback books, perfect binding is both quick and cheap. The finished book will not usually last as long as a book that is edition bound.

the remaining three edges and the cover are flush. Only about 0.3 cm (⅛ inch) is trimmed from the edges of a book which is perfect bound.

A cheap way of producing a hardback book is to perfect bind the sections and then cover them with a hard case, which is a little larger than the pages. But these tend to get slightly damaged when stored on end, because the cover takes the full weight of the book. Another cover variation is a dust jacket, which is an extra sheet of paper wrapped around the book to protect it.

A dust jacket will not only protect the book, it will improve its appearance.

Edition binding

Most hardback books are edition bound, or casebound. The sections are sewn together and a case of board covered with material is made for the book. The case is attached to the sewn sections with strips of tape that have been sewn into the spine of the sections. These strips are covered up with endpapers (the leaves at the front and back of a book covering the inner sides of the case).

This is called a flat back casebound book – because the spine is flat. Often books are simply sewn and stuck to the back of the case without strips being used; endpapers are used to cover the gap between the book and the cover, and to give the book strength. An adhesive strip, called a *crash*, is stuck to the back of the sewn sections to give the book extra strength.

Round back casebound books are made in a similar way: the signatures are sewn together, but then the spine is clamped and hammered round. The case is also clamped on, so that it retains the rounded look to the back of the book. The best books are bound in this way and sometimes headbands are added for decoration, or a book mark ribbon is included at the stage where the crash is glued to the spine of the sewn sections. This is the most expensive form of binding.

Find out the binding options available to you locally and get quotations of prices from both

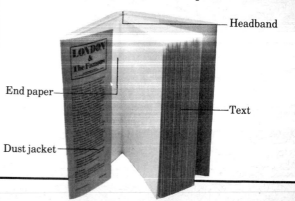

Headband

End paper

Text

Dust jacket

printers and binders. (Printers usually sub-contract binding work out, so it may be cheaper to arrange it yourself.) If you require a book to be casebound the binders usually have a selection of materials and colours to be used on the outside. The endpapers are usually white or cream; coloured or printed papers, which are more expensive, can be used to complement the cover of the book.

Slide binding

This is a form of binding you can do yourself without any machines. Slide binders, in a limited selection of colours, can be bought from most good stationers. You just slide a binder down the side of loose leaf pages to hold them together. If the pages are not thick enough for the binder to grip, fold the left-hand edge of the pages back to double the thickness where the binder is gripping.

Box making and packaging

A book cover, the method of binding and the surface graphics on it, can be thought of as packaging. They serve to protect, as well as enhance, the object despite the fact that they are an integral part of it. Many other objects come in forms which cannot be so readily or elegantly packaged. Bottles, cans, vacuum packs, cartons and boxes are all types of packaging. All of them carry some surface graphics and many are ingeniously crafted pieces of technology.

A whole section of the graphic and printing trade is devoted to packaging, because most manufacturers are prepared to spend large sums of money in order to present their products well. Consequently, if you require a quantity of boxes, you will almost certainly find a company able to make them for you at a reasonable cost. The packager will also be able to give you clear specifications of how to produce the artwork for any surface graphics, and will provide you with some blank boxes to test your ideas on. But for this service you will need to order at least 100 or 150 boxes.

To make your own box, find a box roughly similar to the one you wish to make. Carefully unglue it and examine the way in which it was constructed and from what sort of card. You can then draw out a plan for your box, cut it out of suitable card and glue it together. Remember you will have to allow for the thickness of the board when designing a box which needs to fit the contents snugly. Also, ensure that the glueing flaps are large enough to hold the box together – use your existing box as a guide.

The most difficult part of making a box is glueing it together. While the glue is setting, support the structure to keep the corners square with elastic bands. Alternatively, you can design the box so that it snaps together using tabs and slots. This style is used commercially so that the boxes can be stored flat while awaiting use.

12. MAKING SIGNS AND DISPLAYS

SIGNS

Signs, especially outdoor ones, have to be constructed of a much more solid material than the other graphically designed items described in this book. And, as with posters, the design has only a very short period of time in which to catch and hold the attention of the passer-by.

The main problem with signs is one of scale. Of course, this must also be considered when producing a piece of information that is to be held in the hand and read; but the problem is compounded if you are to view the result from, say, 50 metres (164 feet) (see page 78).

Once the scale is correct, particular skills are needed to execute the sign. Letters are often drawn freehand, but only with extraordinary confidence, especially the ones in calligraphic or decorative style. Fairground lettering is a good example of freehand decorative lettering. Although the lettering is easy enough to read, if you look closely you will see a remarkable amount of detailed work. It takes a long time to acquire such skill.

Assessing your needs

When you are making your own sign it is essential to choose the right materials and design. To do this you need to know whether the sign is to be temporary (one day to one week), semi-permanent (one week to six months), or permanent (anything over six months); whether it is to be placed indoors or outdoors; whether it will be freestanding, or attached to some existing structure; how many signs are needed; and how much money you can spend.

How permanent?
All signs require the use of materials more hardwearing than those used for other graphic products. Even a sign required for only a day must be constructed of material heavier than just paper. Of course, signs can be made of paper and then pasted on to a wall or mounted on board: the wall or board is providing the structure that the paper on its own does not have. But the longer the sign will be needed, the more hardwearing it must be.

Indoors or outdoors?
Obviously if your sign appears outdoors the materials you use, both for the supporting structure and the actual sign, need to be capable of standing up to changes in temperature and weather. Although the construction does not need to be so rigorous if you are working indoors, sometimes there are unusual conditions which must be taken into account. If a sign is to be placed in a greenhouse, for instance, it must be made of materials which are not adversely affected by high levels of temperature and humidity.

Freestanding or attached?
If a sign is to be freestanding and also outdoors, you will have a considerable construction problem on your hands. Materials to use are described on page 152.

There are various ways of anchoring a freestanding sign. To raise it to a suitable height, it must be attached to a post, which is sunk into the ground. If the sign is to be permanent, then it is best to sink the post into concrete; consult an instruction manual for advice on how to do this, or contact your local hardware store.

If an outdoor sign is to be attached to an existing structure rather than freestanding, there are two basic approaches. The first, to build the sign into a wall, is expensive and time consuming, although it does have the advantage of being permanent. If you do choose to fix your sign in this way your local hardware store will again give advice on the best methods.

To attach the sign to a door, a post or other wooden background, use bolts. Screws are the next best method. Nails are not satisfactory; the sign could be too easily removed.

How many are needed?

If you need two or more identical signs, it is worth considering ways of duplicating the signs, rather than making each separately. Stencilling is one of the cheapest, quickest and most effective methods of duplicating signs. For five or more signs, screenprinting becomes economic, saving you both time and materials. If printing or painting, check that the ink or paint you use is compatible with the surface on which it is applied.

If the signs are for indoor use, good quality photocopied prints are suitable, especially if framed. You can use either colour or black and white photocopies, but the sizes available are usually restricted.

If you require ten or more signs which have the letters raised from the background (or in relief), it is economic in terms of both time and materials to produce them in resin or glass fibre laminate. The design can be as complex as you wish, and these materials have the benefit of being at the same time relatively strong and lightweight. The raised letterforms can be emphasized if necessary by painting. The mould for the signs is made out of plaster or wood, and making it is the most time consuming part of this process.

How much money do you wish to spend?

It is possible to produce small, inexpensive indoor signs on paper or card. At the other extreme, it is possible to spend a great deal of money on a sheet of copper which is then suitably prepared for vitreous enamelling. (Even more expensive is chiselled stone or slate. But for these you would certainly have to engage the services of a professional.) For materials, the ascending order of cost is: paper, card, marine plywood, Formica, aluminium, steel, copper.

The techniques used can be similarly graded: photocopying, painting, stencilling, instant lettering, PVC film material and cut-out letters, screenprinting, enamelling.

Materials

For indoor use

Paper can be used if backed with stiff card or wood or if pasted to a wall.

Cardboard can be worked on with paint, instant lettering and self-adhesive colours. But even quite thick card tends to bend; like paper, it needs to be fixed securely to a strong backing.

Hardboard is cheap and, unless used in very large sizes, does not bend as noticeably as card. If you need a freestanding indoor sign, use double-sided hardboard (two sheets of hardboard bonded together), which is available in a thickness of 0.5 cm (¼ inch).

The hardboard should be primed with emulsion paint to the colour you require before the lettering is painted or applied directly on to it. Alternatively, coloured adhesive sheets can be used as background or cut to any desired shape.

Polyboard is a very useful product which is quite stiff and very light. It consists of sheets of rigid paste foam, with smooth paper bonded to both sides. You can work directly on to its surface.

Plywood is stiffest and sturdiest of all, but its slightly rough finish needs priming, and you would benefit from using plastic sheets of colour and lettering to improve the finish.

For outdoor and freestanding signs

Vitreous enamelling on to a steel or copper sheet. This gives a very attractive result, and the range of colours and effects is rich and wide. But the sign must be fired in a suitable kiln or oven, which makes it an expensive procedure.

Aluminium sheet using plastic adhesive sheets and letters for the graphics. This, too, is expensive.

Formica laminated on to a baseboard. Like aluminium, Formica takes plastic film and pre-cut letters very well, and is less expensive than the aluminium.

Plywood; you must use waterproofed marine ply coated with one or two layers of varnish (melamine lacquer is best, but household polyurethane will do). Do not use plastic films or letters, or instant lettering, as these will weather away from this surface. Screenprinting or painting with signwriter's paint is best. Further coats of clear varnish must be applied to the finished sign for final weather proofing. Marine ply is cheaper than enamelling, aluminium or Formica.

Lettering

There is a vast range of cut-out lettering (flat or relief) in a constantly widening range of materials and finishes, which can be bought from art supply stores. It is difficult to cut your own letters from cork, and even more so with harder materials, but try cutting letters from a poly-styrene sheet with a hot-wire cutting tool. A simpler technique is mask-cutting. Make a stencil by cutting letters out of an adhesive material. You can then stick the background down on to your surface, paint over the cut-out areas, leave to dry and then peel off the adhesive. The letters remain behind in coloured paint. Alternatively, do the reverse: stick the letters down on to the surface in the position required. Paint over the whole surface, allow to dry and then peel off the letters, leaving the original background colour for your letterforms.

Making a sign

A permanent car park sign

First decide on the information to be given. In most cases the words CAR PARK with perhaps an arrow will be sufficient. Think about the intended location for the sign. This will determine the size of the lettering (by its distance from the reader), the colours (to provide a reasonable contrast to its surroundings) and, of course, the direction of the arrow.

Now decide how the information should be laid out and find a source for the characters that will appear on the sign (simple capital letters are best). Newspaper headlines and advertisements provide a good source – so may a poster or similar printed material. If you fail to find such a source you could produce an original from dry transfer lettering and have an enlarged print made to the size you required by a local photoprinter (see your local classified telephone directory).

Use an accurate tracing of the information to go on to the sign, work out a suitable size for the board and cut it from plywood or sheet metal. Prime the signboard and then give it two coats of undercoat (no top coat is needed). This colour should stand out from the predominant colour of the setting in which it will be viewed. When the paint is thoroughly dry, tape down the tracing of the design in the correct position and place a piece of carbon paper face down beneath it. Trace the image firmly so that the shape is transferred.

Once the image has been marked onto the sign board it can be painted in. Use a contrasting colour to the board itself. The most readable colours are black, white and yellow. Using a fine artist's brush, slowly paint along the edge of each shape. Concentrate on making the outside edge as clean and as smooth as possible. Rotate either the board or yourself so that you are always in the most comfortable position to paint. Once the edges are complete fill in the rest of the shape with a larger, flat-ended brush. Sign writing is a highly skilled job so work slowly to give yourself the best chance of producing a professional finish. Apply the paint more thickly than you would for a large area so as to avoid the necessity for two coats. Once dry give the whole sign two coats of glossy, clear varnish and mount the sign in the most visible position using non-rusting screws.

ART CENTER COLLEGE OF DESIGN LIBRARY
1700 LIDA STREET
PASADENA, CALIFORNIA 91103

MAKING SIGNS AND DISPLAY

An indoor sign

As indoor signs need not be weatherproof a wide variety of construction materials are available. Your choice will largely depend on the degree of permanence and how smart it needs to be. The simplest can be handwritten on paper or card (using a felt tip pen) and pinned or taped to a suitable structure. (To protect decorations use masking tape or Blu-Tack.) If you need more than one sign, photocopy the original.

If you need greater permanence and higher quality, buy pressure-sensitive sticky letters. They have adhesive applied to the reverse which is protected by backing paper. The letters come in a range of sizes and several colours, but the larger sizes are quite expensive. This instant lettering is useful for exhibition signs and displays, where white or coloured board can be used as the base. They are easy to use and their arrangement can be arranged before the backing paper is removed.

You may want to include images as well as lettering on your sign. Photoprinting allows a piece of artwork to be blown-up and the resulting photographic print can be mounted on board or other materials to make an attractive sign. Produce the artwork as you would for offset printing (see pages 120-7). You are less likely, however, to be working at the final size; and remember that the bigger the enlargement the more any imperfections in the artwork will be apparent.

Prepare the artwork and give it to the photoprinter with precise instructions as to size, reversing and mounting. (Photoprinters are usually listed in classified telephone directories). If you ask for it to be mounted it will be delivered to you ready to hang. For sticking to a vertical surface use Velcro pads, double-sided tape, push pins etc., but be careful when removing the sign. It could also be hung from a structure on strong thread or cord attached to adhesive picture hanging eyes.

A TEMPORARY SHOP FASCIA SIGN

Shop fascia boards tend to be large and inaccessible. Professionals usually draw hand lettering on poster paper, and then paste the letters to the fascia board. Although by no means an easy method this is probably the best approach for the amateur as well.

Firstly measure the size of the fascia board and draw it to a scale that will fit on to an ordinary drawing pad. Sketch out a number of designs until you find the one you want. Bear in mind that you must allow for the thickness of the letters, and also that the simpler the sign the better the final result is likely to be. Do not aim to reproduce faithfully a typeface you have seen on a printed page – go for a simple letter form of equal width throughout.

Poster paper is available in various sizes (the most common being 500×600 mm (20×30 inch)) and in various colours including fluorescent colours. Try artshops or a local poster writer who may be persuaded to let you have a few sheets. Buy enough to cover the area of the fascia board and some to spare.

Find sufficient floor space to lay out the sheets so that they cover the same area as the fascia. Try to use as few sheets as possible. Tape them lightly together and then to the floor with masking tape.

Now indicate on the sketch of your chosen design the size and position of the sheets of poster paper that you have assembled on the floor.

Remember to work to the same scale as your sketch. Returning to the poster paper, lightly draw two horizontal guide lines to show the top and bottom of each line of typematter. Start to sketch the letterforms on to the paper using chalk, referring constantly to your scale sketch and brushing out the chalk marks each time you make a mistake. Build up the whole sign letter by letter until you are happy with the spacing, then go back and put in the detail of each letter-form. Frequently stand back and ensure that the shapes and spacings are correct.

Once you are satisfied with the outlines of the characters, paint them in using poster colour and a suitable brush. Try to create each letter with as few strokes as possible using relaxed flowing movements. The brush width will depend on the width of the letters.

Once the sign is complete trim away any excess paper and paste the letters into position using ordinary wallpaper paste. Be sure to take care when pasting the sign into position. Use a properly secured ladder and a 100 or 150 mm (4 or 6 inch) brush to distribute the paste.

DISPLAY

Display surfaces
Walls
Material can be taped to walls, either with masking tape or double sided tape, but both methods tend to damage painted surfaces. Light materials can be stuck to walls with any proprietary brand of tacky putty. Contrary to makers' claims, though, this adhesive tends to leave marks, not only on walls but also on the display article. However, it is easy to use and economical.

Boards
There are a number of types of boards which can be used for display purposes. If work is to be pinned directly on to it a soft type made from compressed fibre is best, but if it is to be painted and used as a base on to which material will be glued, probably a smooth faced board would be better. These range from paper-based to wood-based products. Both soft and hardfaced boards can be covered with fabric or paper although the soft variety is probably easier to deal with. Soft board covered with hessian or felt makes a very effective display surface. Pull the fabric lightly over the front and staple it securely at the back. (For public displays use fire resistant fabrics.)

Apart from the type of surface the two most important factors in choosing board are weight and rigidity. Choose the lightest possible for ease of handling and cost. Rigidity is less important if the boards are to be mounted on a firm structure.

Use pins, staple guns, adhesives, adhesive tape or velcro to attach displays to the board.

Polystyrene flats
Polystyrene is available in a large variety of shapes and sizes. It is easy to cut and very light and can be used in a similar way to board.

Although not as long lasting as board, it is excellent for short-life exhibitions.

Cardboard boxes
These can be covered with lining paper, then painted and used as units to construct display stands.

Island units can be made simply from creasing and folding flat sheets of various light-weight materials including cardboard and compressed fibre board. There are many designs which can be put to a wide variety of display applications.

By making use of glued tabs, more sophisticated shapes can be made. Open ended cubes, cylinders, hexagons etc. make attractive multidisplay surfaces.

The traditional show card is also easy to make.

Wooden boxes
Sturdier than cardboard boxes, these can have paint applied directly to them, and can be used to support quite substantial weights. Alternatively they can be covered in cloth or paper. Be careful to remove dangerous nails or staples used to hold the box together.

Manufactured systems
Storage system units, usually made of chipboard and available in kit form, are pressed together using interlocking metal pins. These are then fixed in position with a circular key. You can construct quite large complex and permanent shelfing areas with no prior knowledge of carpentry, and no tools.

System framing
These are metal 'skeleton' systems. From a number of struts, screws and bolts and a metal saw, you can construct a rigid framework to any design, just add chipboard or plywood for shelving and panelling, or fit specially manufactured metal shelves. One disadvantage is that you do need a few tools.

INDEX

ART CENTER COLLEGE OF DESIGN LIBRARY
1700 LIDA STREET
PASADENA, CALIFORNIA 91103